Learning Social Science at Upper Primary Level

D.El.Ed.-509

For

Diploma in Elementary Education [D.El.Ed.]

IMPORTANT STUDY MATERIAL FOR NIOS, SCERT, B.El.Ed. (DU), DIET, JBT, IGNOU

GULLYBABA PUBLISHING HOUSE PVT. LTD.
ISO 9001 & ISO 14001 CERTIFIED CO.

Developed and Produced by:

GullyBaba Publishing House Pvt. Ltd.

Regd. Office:
2525/193, 1ˢᵗ Floor, Onkar Nagar-A,
Tri Nagar, Delhi-110035
(From Kanhaiya Nagar Metro Station Towards
Old Bus Stand)
Ph. 011-27387998, 27384836, 27385249

Branch Office:
1A/2A, 20, Hari Sadan,
Ansari Road, Daryaganj,
New Delhi-110002
Ph. 011-23289034
011-45794768

E-mail: hello@gullybaba.com, **Website:** GullyBaba.com
First Edition: 2018

Author: Gullybaba.Com Panel
ISBN: 978-93-86276-79-7

Free Home Delivery of GPH Books

To get the books by VPP/COD, Email/SMS your complete address, telephone number, subject code of the books.

You can also send your order through WhatsApp on 09350849407.

To get the books by RBD/Speed Post/Courier, Pay in advance by Bank Draft (in favour of "Gullybaba Publishing House (P) Ltd.")/ Money Order/ Online Transfer/Cash Deposit. In case of DD/Cheque add ₹25 extra. In case of cash deposit, add ₹110 extra in total. And email your payment details.

Free Shipping in India only for orders above `500/-

Order online through GullyBaba.com.

For more information dial:- 09350849407, 09312235086, or email us at gphbooks@gullybaba.com.

Preface

The social sciences carry a normative responsibility to create and widen the popular base for human values, namely freedom, trust, mutual respect, respect for diversity, etc. Thus, social science teaching basically should be aimed at investing in a child a moral and mental energy so as to provide her with the ability to think independently and deal with the social forces that threaten these values, without losing her individuality. Social Science teaching can achieve this by promoting children's ability to take initiative to critically reflect on social issues that have a bearing on the creative coexistence between individual good and collective good. Critical reflection pre-supposes a comprehensive curriculum in which learners – both teachers and children – participate in generating knowledge without any latent and manifest forces of coercion. It is through this non-coercive and participatory mode that children and teachers stand the best chance of making teaching and learning interesting as well as enjoyable.

The disciplines that make up the social sciences, namely history, geography, political science and economics, have distinct methodologies that often justify the preservation of boundaries. The boundaries of disciplines need to be opened up and a plurality of approaches may be applied to understand a given phenomenon. For an enabling curriculum, certain themes that facilitate interdisciplinary thinking are required.

The contents of social Science/social studies as a school subject are based on a certain understanding about their nature and purposes. Instead of treating these as natural and given, this GPH book *"Learning Social Science at Upper Primary Level (D.El.Ed.-509)"* introduces student-teachers to different perspectives about these subjects. It would also examine the ways in which different visions and understanding of the subjects get reflected in different curriculum, syllabus and textbooks. The book asks and suggests how social sciences can develop capacities to critically understand society and social reality around us with reference to time, space and power, structures, institutions, processes and relationships.

The book is written specially in question & answer format to provide students the instant gratification of a correct answer. In this book, we have tried to solve all possible questions from the exams' point of view. Solutions of previous years' question papers have also been included to help you to understand the unique examination structure. We hope that this book would not only be a favourite study material for the students but also can be a nice resource for teaching.

An attempt has been carefully made to present this book more useful and meet the requirements and challenges of the course prescribed by University/Institution.

We wish you a successful and rewarding career ahead. Feedback in this regard is solicited.

— Gullybaba.Com Panel

Acknowledgement

Our compliments go to the **GullyBaba Publishing House Pvt. Ltd.,** and its meticulous team who have been enthusiastically working towards the perfection of the book.

Their teamwork, initiative and research have been very encouraging. Had it not been for their unflagging support, this work wouldn't have been possible. The creative freedom provided by them along with their aim of presenting the best to the reader has been a major source of inspiration in this work. Hope that this book would be successful.

—Gullybaba.Com Panel

Publisher's Note

The present book D.El.Ed.-509 is targeted for examination purpose as well as enrichment. With the advent of technology and the Internet, there has been no dearth of information available to all; however, finding the relevant and qualitative information, which is focussed, is an uphill task.

We, at **GullyBaba Publishing House Pvt. Ltd.,** have taken this step to provide quality material which can accentuate in-depth knowledge about the subject. GPH books are a pioneer in the effort of providing unique and quality material to its readers. With our books, you are sure to attain success by making use of this powerful study material. Provided book is just a reference book based on the syllabus of particular University/Board. For a profound information, see the textbooks recommended by the University/Board.

Our site **gullybaba.com** is a vital resource for your examination. The publisher wishes to acknowledge the significant contribution of the Team Members and our experts in bringing out this publication and highly thankful to Almighty God, without His blessings, this endeavour wouldn't have been successful.

– Publisher

Topics Covered

Contents

Question Papers

Understanding Social Science as a Discipline

INTRODUCTION

Social sciences constitute a branch/field of knowledge which basically studies human affairs or human relationship in the spectrum of broad social system. Social sciences emerged as the formal subjects of study in the eighteenth century in response to meet the social problems and challenges that are created by the development of modern science, industrialisation, modernisation, etc. Realising the importance of social sciences for developing democratic and social citizenship qualities among young learners, since last century social sciences have been the part of school curriculum in almost all the countries of the Globe including our country India. Social sciences as a field of study includes large number of subjects like political science, anthropology, law, economics, geography, etc. After independence, new values and aspirations found reflection in the constitution of India. Values such as socialism, secularism, liberty, equality, justice, and fraternity found expression in the new social sciences curriculum. The new social sciences curriculum also took note of issues like diversity, national integration, international understanding, environment, development, etc.

Q1. Describe the evolution of social sciences.

Ans. The revival of interest in social science occurred in the middle of the 18th century. By the middle of 18th century, capitalism had begun to outgrow its early state and gradually it became the dominant socio-economic system in western and northern Europe.

The evolution and growth of social sciences are the byproduct of modernisation, industrialisation, renaissance, urbanisation, growth of science and many more related developments. There were many changes in human lives and living, which were hardly seen before during the eighteenth century and afterwards. The whole world took a radical turn since the eighteenth century. Renaissance in Italy and other European countries, French revolution 1789, industrial revolutions starting from 1767, American war of independence 1776, development of new forms of capitalism, immense development in natural sciences, etc. brought both happiness and difficulties for human society in the world. For example, on the positive side, there was commercial development, development of transport and communication, multiplication of comforts, improvement of education and health condition, development of economic condition, etc.; and on the negative side, there was development of complexity in social life, political chaos, social disorganization and unrest, intellectual crisis, development of unhealthy competition among people, etc. In order to counter all these problems and challenges, social sciences originated and became the part of education/ learning system.

In an effort to understand the character and future of modern society, social sciences come into view in the 18th century. During observing the difference between modern society and its feudal and ancient forms, various social scientists envisioned social sciences that would guide modern society into the future.

Indefinable misery for mankind was brought by two wars (i.e. World War-I and World war-II) in the twentieth. In addition to these two wars, there were/are numerous wars which were/are found in many parts of the world which were/are really bad for humanity. The misuse of science, urbanisation, industrialisation etc. has really become a threat to humanity in this world. The experience of severe economic depression from 1930 to 1940 created the feeling of insecurity, fear, suspicion and distrust among the people of the world. The rapid growth of science and technology in the last hundred years has created many new social problems, though it has many positive effects. Social sciences emerged to prevent and check the evil effects of science, industrialization and modernization, etc. on the one hand and to guide the modern society for better future on the other hand.

For modern day society, social sciences have great relevance. They form an important component/part of modern day education/curriculum system. Social sciences have become the part of university/higher education system across the world starting from the eighteenth century.

Q2. Discuss the concept of social science and social studies.

Ans. Concept of Social Science: According to Charles Beard Social Sciences are a body of Knowledge and thought pertaining to human affairs as distinguished from sticks, stones, stars and physical objects. James High defines the Social Sciences as those bodies of learning and study which recognise the simultaneous and mutual action of physical and non-physical stimuli which produce social reaction.

Thus, the term social sciences may include any disciplined knowledge which deals with people and utilises a scientific method.

Social Sciences include history, geography, political science, economics, anthropology and sociology which represent man's fundamental needs: the human record, habitat, political structure, subsistence, human, derivation and social organisation. Human or cultural geography and psychology account for human needs of acceptance and personal adjustment. Social Sciences may also include social biology, ethics, philosophy, jurisprudence, statistics, linguistics and education, and even rhetoric, logic and grammar.

The following points characterise the nature of social sciences:

(1) Social sciences are basically concerned with human relationship. Study of the nature of human society is the ultimate goal of all social sciences.

(2) Social sciences study mostly the social issues, and social issues are always more complex, more subjective and less verifiable than the issues of physical sciences.

(3) Social sciences have their own/distinct content areas and methodologies for approaching and understanding knowledge. Some of the common methods used in social sciences for understanding knowledge are historical, thematic, participatory, non-coercive, quasi experimental, etc.

(4) Concern for value attainment is an important tenet of social sciences. Therefore, social scientists bother always for goodness or value of something that they attain or deal with.

(5) Social sciences are primarily interdisciplinary in nature. A concept or issue of social sciences may not be confined to one discipline of social sciences, rather the concept or the issue may be understood taking into account the perspectives of all disciplines of social sciences.

(6) Social sciences facilitate plurality in thinking in understanding an issue. Since in social situation a single effect has numerous causes and a single cause has numerous effects, so, social sciences facilitate multiple thinking referring to a single issue.

Concept of Social Studies: Social studies reveals to the learner where s/he is in the context of time, space and society. Hence, definitions and the nature of social studies range from a study of human beings favouring a separate subject approach to an integrated one in which the subject matter is indistinguishable as history, geography, civics and so on.

In 1992, the Board of Directors of National Council for the Social Studies, the primary membership organization for social studies educators, adopted the following definition: Social studies is the integrated study of the social sciences and humanities to promote civic competence. Within the school program, social studies provides coordinated, systematic study drawing upon such disciplines as anthropology, archaeology, economics, geography, history, law, philosophy, political science, psychology, religion, and sociology, as well as appropriate content from the humanities, mathematics, and natural sciences. The primary purpose of social studies is to help young people develop the ability to make informed and reasoned decisions for the public good as citizens of a culturally diverse, democratic society in an interdependent world.

Some definitions of Social Studies are as follows:

According to the Council of Social Studies of U.S.A- "In Social Studies the subjects included are the subject which are concerned with the development of Human Construction and the organisation of Human Structure."

According to John Jarolimeck-"Social Studies, studies the social subjects relating to environment and person."

According to John U. Mchelis-"Social Studies, studies the actions relating to environment and the human beings."

According to E.B. Wesley-"Social Studies points out to the subject material whose basic elements are Social."

According to J.F. Forrester-"Social Studies as its name shows, it is the studies of Society, its main objectives is to help the students to understand them the Environment in which they live so that they may be a responsible citizen."

Thus, Social Studies develops the key values and attitudes, knowledge and understanding, and skills and processes necessary for students to become active and responsible citizens, engaged in the democratic process and aware of their capacity to effect change in their communities, society and world.

The following points may characterize the nature of social studies:

(1) Social studies are concerned with human study in relation to socio-cultural environment.

(2) Social studies have been evolved from social sciences as an instructional area in order to be taught at school level for promoting healthy social/democratic living among learners.

(3) Social studies establish the relationship among present, past and future.

(4) Social studies stress more on contemporary human life and its problems than the past history of man.

(5) Social studies aims at enabling students to adjust to their socio-cultural environment which includes family, community, state, nation and at large the entire humanity.

(6) Social studies are a realistic course or deals with practical aspects of society.

(7) Social studies are now at growing and developing stage. It is trying to make its scope broader and wider.

(8) Social studies are considered now as a core subject at school level for developing necessary competencies relating to healthy social living.

Q3. Elucidate functional similarities and differences between social sciences and social studies.

Or

Define the relationship between Social Studies and Social Science in two points. [April-2016, Q.No.-31]

Or

Write any *five* differences between Social Science and Social Studies at upper primary level.[April-2016, Q.No.-42]

Ans. Social studies and social science can be easy to confuse. The two terms have different meanings so that they cannot be used interchangeably.

Social sciences and social studies have many similarities also. They are not only related generally but also share a common body of content. The social sciences are the parent disciplines. The centre of focus in social sciences and social studies is man's relationship to man his environment and how he meets his needs. Human relationships are the common denominators. As a matter of fact there is no hard and fast line separating social studies in the primary and middle classes where gradual unfolding of the total environment physical, social and cultural is needed. As the student gains more insight and becomes mature to interpret raw data at the secondary and higher secondary stages, he emerges from the social studies and enters into social sciences.

Some common similarities are as follows:

(1) Human relationship is the common denominator in case of both social sciences and social studies.

(2) Both focus on woman/man engaging in variety of activities for the purpose of meeting her/her basic needs, communicating her/his ideas and feelings, producing and consuming the necessities of life and saving human and natural resources.

(3) Both of them share a common body of course contents.

(4) In case of both, the central focus is woman's/man's relationship with woman/ man and her/his environment.

Some of the differences between both are as follows:

(1) Social sciences are the advanced studies of human society which are taught at the high school stage, higher secondary stage and at college stage. Social studies are simplified portions of social sciences selected for instructional purposes at the primary and middle stages.

(2) Social sciences represent an adult approach while the social studies represent a child-centred approach.

(3) Social sciences are the theory part of human affairs and social studies as the practical part of human affairs.

(4) Social sciences lay more emphasis on knowledge and social studies on the functional part of knowledge.

(5) Social sciences are concerned with the investigation of a diversity of human relations and pile up considerably more data than it is possible or desirable to include in social studies.

(6) Social sciences aim at finding out how new truth about human relationship and social studies aim at guiding adolescents in their learning of selected portions of what has been discovered in social sciences.

Q4. State the position of social sciences in present school curriculum of India.

Ans. Social science is a common core subject for all primary, lower secondary and upper secondary education programmes. Learning in the subject shall therefore be made as relevant as possible for pupils by adapting the subject to the different education programmes.

In India, at the lower primary school level (i.e., class I-V), social sciences are taught to the learners as the part of environmental studies or environmental sciences curriculum. At the upper primary school level (i.e. class VI-VIII) and secondary school level (i.e. Class IX and X), social sciences are taught to the learners as a core composite instructional area of curriculum, and this area of curriculum is called as 'social studies' or 'social sciences'. At the upper primary and the secondary school levels mainly three to four instructional subjects/components (for example, history, geography etc.) comprise the social sciences/ social studies curriculum. At the higher secondary school level (i.e. class XI and XII), different social science subjects like political science, anthropology, economics, psychology, etc. are taught to the learners as the optional/specialized courses.

The term 'social sciences' and 'social studies', to a great extent, are interchangeably used at the upper primary and/or the secondary levels. For example, NCF (2005, p-53) used the term 'social studies' in the context of curriculum of the upper primary stage, whereas, the Position Paper – Nation Focus Group on Teaching Social Sciences (2006, p-5) has used the term 'social sciences' in the context of curriculum of the upper primary stage. In the text books of 'history', 'geography' and 'social and political life' at upper primary level of CBSE curriculum (published by NCERT) the term 'social science' is used. Whatever the terms (i.e. 'social studies' or 'social sciences') used, the focus of teaching learning of 'social sciences' (or 'social studies') changes according to the levels of education that is already discussed earlier. At school level, learning of social studies/ social sciences focuses on the issues which are functionally different from the issues of learning of social sciences at higher education level.

Q5. Explain the prevailing nature of social sciences in pre-modern, and modern and contemporary world.

Ans. Pre-modern world experienced many phases of human civilisation ranging from hunting gathering age, pastoral nomadic age, Stone Age, Iron Age, river valley civilisations and medieval age to eighteenth/nineteenth century. Since the days when the human beings put their feet in this world and established the family/society, understanding of society/social system became necessary for them. Therefore, there was a necessity of learning social sciences. In those days, the learning of social sciences was informal and unorganised one. As day by day the human society became complex and social demands and challenges multiplied, accordingly the study of social sciences became a necessity.

Socrates Plato, Aristotle and many more intellectuals of the ancient world contributed a lot to social sciences. Plato's 'Republic' and Aristotle's 'Politics' are ever memorable works in the field of social sciences. The idea/learning of social sciences was embodied in the Civic oath of the Greeks, when they were admitted to citizenship on attainment of maturity, they would take an oath in the formal ceremony. In the mediaeval and early modern world, large number of subjects which have wide implication for attainment of social values like religious studies, economics and business studies, studies of state affairs etc. became the part of education system.

Social sciences in modern and contemporary world: In the modern age as new social problems are generating day by day, accordingly new social sciences are emerging to solve/mitigate such problems. Social sciences have become the formal component of higher education/ university curriculum since the eighteenth century and have become formal component of school curriculum since the twentieth century. Especially after two world wars, social sciences have got high importance in school curriculum in most parts of the world. In post world war periods, most of the international bodies relating to education like the UNESCO, the UNICEF, the UNDP, the UNO, etc. want to promote healthy social living among the people of the world, which ultimately emphasizes learning of social sciences. Art-1 of Universal Declarations of Human Rights (1948) adopted by the United Nation states, *"All human being are born free and equal in dignity and rights. They are endowed with reason and conscience, and should act towards one another in a spirit of brotherhood"*. Delores Commission (1996) stresses a lot on learning to live together. For promoting the virtues of living together harmoniously and solving the diverse socio-cultural problems of the modern world, social sciences have become a significant part of formal and non-formal education of the modern world. Further, the creation of nation states and the practice of democratic and socialistic model of governance in such nation states in most part of the contemporary world have made the learning of social sciences necessary at both school and university level, because social sciences take the responsibility to create effective citizens for the practice of democratic and socialistic governance in the nation states.

Q6. Discuss the Indian perspectives of social sciences in different ages.

Or

Explain the place of social sciences learning in ancient Indian cultural/educational system.

Ans. Vedas, Upanishads, Smritis, Puranas, Ramayana, Mahabharata etc. are some of the pre-historic/early-historic Indian scriptures which bear social values and healthy living principles. The 'Arthashastra' of Kautilya, Panchatantra of Vishnu Sharma etc. are some of the ancient Indian compositions or texts which deal with social science tenets and principles. The early medieval and medieval literary traditions like Buddhist texts,

Jain texts, Islamic texts, Bhakti texts, etc. are one way or other considered as texts of social and cultural values and heritage. Referring to all these contexts, we can say social sciences had become the part of Indian education and culture system both in the ancient and the medieval time. Following points describe how school level social sciences are treated by plans and policies of education from time to time:

The Secondary Education Commission (1952-53) remarks: "Social studies as a term, is comparatively new in Indian education. It is meant to cover the ground traditionally associated with history, geography, economics, civics etc……This whole group of studies has, therefore, to be viewed as compact whole whose object is to adjust the students to their social environment- which includes the family, community, state and nation – so that they may be able to understand how society has come to its present form and interpret intelligently the matrix of social forces and movement in the midst of which they are living".

The Education Commission (1964-66) remarks: "The aim of teaching social studies is to help the students acquire knowledge of their environment, an understanding of human relationship, and attitude and values which are vital for intelligent participation in the affairs of the community, the state, the nation and the world. An effective programme of social studies is essential in India for development of good citizenship and emotional integration".

'The Curriculum For Ten Year School: A Framework' of NCERT (1975) remarks: "Environmental studies will include both natural and social environment in class I and II. It will be more appropriate to use the term social studies rather than social sciences at primary stage, since it represents a broad and composite instructional area."

National Curriculum For Elementary And Secondary Education (1988) observes: "Social Science is perhaps the singular curricular area which can prove to be the most effective tool for providing education in the context of all the core-components envisaged by NPE (1986)." The core-components envisaged by NPE are:

(1) History of India's freedom movement
(2) Constitutional obligations
(3) Values such as India's common cultural heritage
(4) Egalitarianism, democracy, secularism
(5) Equality of sexes
(6) Protection of environment
(7) Small family norms etc.

National Curriculum Frameworks (2005, P-50) remarks: "The social sciences encompass diverse concerns of society, and include a wide range of content drawn from the disciplines of history, geography, political science, economics, sociology and anthropology. Social science perspectives and knowledge are indispensable to building the knowledge base for a just and peaceful society. The content should aim at raising students' awareness through critically exploring and questioning of familiar social reality. The possibilities of including new dimensions and concerns, especially in view of students' own life experiences, are considerable. Selecting and organizing material into a meaningful curriculum, one that will enable students to develop a critical understanding of society, is therefore a challenging task."

Q7. Enlist and explain current social phenomena and challenges.

Ans. The following points may characterize the current social system and phenomena:

(1) Today, society is a fast growing society based on rapid development of science and technology.

(2) Complexity, heterogeneity, diversity and differentiation in many spheres of life (i.e. economic, political, cultural, religious, etc.) characterize the current society.

(3) New social orders like modernization, industrialization, urbanization, specialization, automation, globalization, privatization, liberalization, planned development, etc. are the basic features of current society.

(4) New social values like democracy, socialism, secularism, liberty, equality, fraternity, justice, scientific temper, individual right, freedom, rationalistic thinking, etc. are the outcomes of modern social system.

(5) Wide range of social mobility, multiculturalism, cultural pluralism, multilingualism, decline of ill social traditions, etc. are rampant in modern society.

(6) Current society faces large number of new social problems and challenges like poverty, unemployment, exploitation based on capitalism, rural-urban difference, development of slums, social alienation, population problem, family disorganization, social crimes, black marketing, social unrest, regionalism, underdevelopment, environmental torturing, problem to cope with information and knowledge explosion, etc.

Q8. What is the scope of social sciences in various disciplines of society? Explain.

Or

Discuss the scope of social sciences learning in the context of current social phenomena and challenges.

Ans. By scope, we mean the extent, variety, depth, breadth and comprehensiveness of learning experience possible through its curriculum transaction. Thus, the scope at Social Science is defined by the range of content and experiences that are to be provided to the learner through its teaching. Scholars like Michaels are of the opinion that the breadth of Social Science programme should provide for a variety of experience so that the child learning will be well rounded and well balanced. It should also be possible to draw upon other fields of learning so that all significant problems can be considered in the light of their many ramifications: a narrow compartmentalized programme is sure to limit the scope of social learning.

As the present society is changing at a faster speed because of the impact of science and technology, advanced media and many more things, new social problems are cropping up day by day. Accordingly, new social sciences are emerging and becoming the part of education system in order to address to such new social problems. In the eighteenth and the nineteenth centuries, social science subjects like social works, public administration, criminology, psychology and demography etc. had little existence, but, in the last and present centuries, these subjects are getting due importance because many new social problems are associated with them. For example, in the eighteenth and even in the nineteenth century, issues relating to population especially growth of population were not major social issues, but in the last and present centuries, the complexities relating to the population growth have affected many aspects of social life for which the subject demography has emerged as the important part of education system. In the pre-modern/early modern societies, the life of the people was simple and the criminal activities were less, but, in the modern industrial society, the criminal activities are found in every sphere of human life. And for checking all the maladies relating to criminal activities, the social science subject 'criminology' has emerged and has become an important part of education system. Likewise, many social science subjects are emerging day by day in order to meet the changing nature of social problems. Therefore, the scope of social sciences is widening gradually.

Q9. Enumerate the subjects considered under social sciences family.

Ans. As the name itself suggests, Social Science is concerned about society. It aims at understanding all aspects of society as well as finding solutions to deal with social problems. It is a broad area of knowledge and includes several different disciplines under its domain.

A branch of knowledge in order to be called as a field of study must fulfill certain conditions. The three major conditions which characterise the nature of a field of study are given under the following three points:

(1) A field must include a number of individual subjects

(2) There exist functional relationship and difference among the subjects under a field.

(3) There exist functional relationships and differences among the different fields or subjects of different fields.

As a branch of knowledge, social sciences fulfill these three conditions in order to be called as a field of study. *Firstly*, social sciences include a large number of individual subjects like history, geography, political science, economics, law etc. *Secondly*, social science subjects are related with each other because human relationship is a common denominator of all the social science subjects. Further difference is marked among all the social science subjects. *Thirdly*, social sciences field and/ or subjects of social sciences field have functional relationship and differences with other fields and/or subjects of other fields. Since all the fields of study are branches of knowledge and knowledge is primarily a unitary concept/phenomenon, so, social sciences field or subjects of social sciences field possesses/posses many characteristics which are common to other fields and/or subjects of other fields. While social science subjects study the social relationships; physical science subjects study physical matters/objects/activities like the currents, heats, lights, chemicals etc.; biological science subjects study the life of animals and plants; mathematical science subjects study the number system and related concepts and the like.

The social science subjects may be categorised under the following three branches/ headings:

- **Pure Social Sciences:** Political science, economics, history, jurisprudence, law, sociology, public administration, social work, human rights, anthropology, etc.
- **Semi Social Sciences:** Ethics, education, philosophy, psychology, art, etc.
- **Sciences with Social Implication:** Geography, biology, medicine, linguistics.

Q10. Identify the instructional components of social sciences at school level.

Ans. School level social studies (or social sciences) curriculum selects its contents from large number of social sciences. In order to be taught to the school students, such selected contents are organised few subject areas, namely, history, geography, etc. of a single and unified umbrella of social studies (or social sciences). For upper primary school level, the present social sciences curriculum of **CBSE** (Published by NCERT) includes three subject areas i.e. **history, geography, and social and political life (SPL).** Similarly, the present social sciences curriculum of **CBSE** (published by NCERT) at secondary school level includes four subject areas i.e. **history, geography, political science and economics.** And at higher secondary level, large number of social science subjects like **history, political science, anthropology, sociology etc.** are taught as specialized/independent subjects.

Different instructional subjects/components of social sciences at upper primary and secondary school stage are presented in below figure:

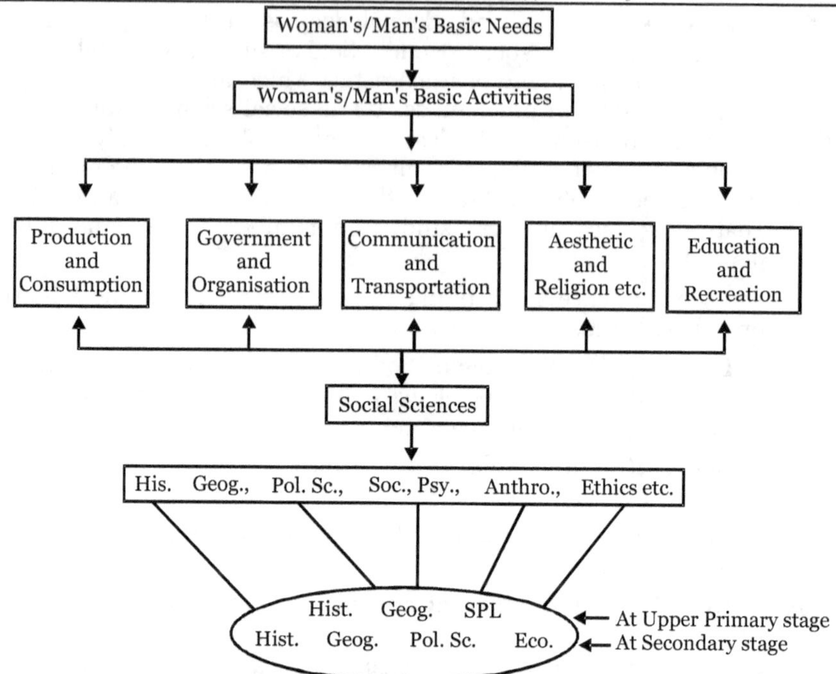

Fig. 1.1: Instructional subjects/components of social sciences at upper primary and secondary stage

Q11. Explain the interdisciplinary and integration perspectives in social sciences.

Ans. Interdisciplinary Perspectives in Social Sciences

Social studies is inherently interdisciplinary. Within the field, the various disciplines that comprise social studies link and intertwine. It's difficult to imagine studying historical content without examining the roles of persons (sociology), their motivations (psychology), where they lived (geography), the influences of spiritual beliefs (religion), rules that govern behavior (political science and anthropology), or how people negotiate for their needs and wants (economics). Outside the field of social studies, vital connections can also be made to language arts, mathematics, science and the arts that yield a deeper understanding of concepts and ideas.

Integrating the concepts or issues of social sciences with the concepts or issues of other disciplines like mathematics, general sciences, languages, etc. is an example of interdisciplinary approach to integration of concepts or issues of social sciences. The social science concept 'money' can be integrated with other disciplines for teaching learning purpose. Students may be asked to compose an essay relating to money. This is an example of integration between social sciences and languages. Many mathematical sums and puzzles relating to money may be presented in front of students. This is an example of integration between social sciences and mathematics. Relating to money, songs can be composed and this indicates the interdisciplinary relationship between social sciences and arts. Like money, many other social science concepts can be integrated with different disciplines in order to facilitate interdisciplinary relationship of social sciences with other disciplines. The following figure depicts interdisciplinary relationship of the social science concept 'money' with other disciplines.

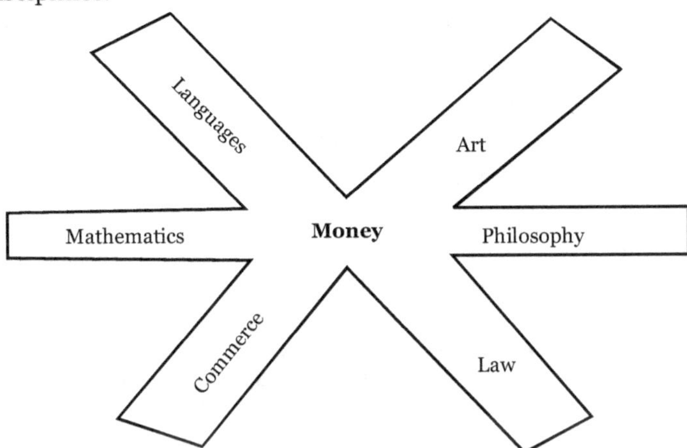

Fig. 1.2: Interdisciplinary Approach to the Social Sciences with the Concept of 'Money'

Integration Perspective in Social Sciences: Integrated curriculum came into focus in the school system with the introduction of Social Studies in to the school curriculum. Integrated curriculum is considered more effective on students compared to single subject approach.

Food, clothing, shelter, transportation, communication, etc. are the common learning concepts of social sciences curriculum at school level. For example, 'Food' can be co-related with subjects of different fields in the following way. The production, marketing, consumption, etc. of food are related to economics; food style, rituals of food, misunderstanding created in family and society because of food, etc. are related to sociology; equality in distribution, budgeting, increase and decrease of price rate, etc. of food are related to political science; issues related to food in different ages, types of food available in different ages, etc. are related to history; preparation of foods of different flavor, maintenance of hygienic habits concerning food, etc. are related to home science; quantification, division, fraction, etc. of food are related to mathematics; types of vitamins and nutrition available in food, categorisation of food items according to their nutritional compositions, etc. are related to life sciences; neatness, cleanness and balancing of diets, etc. of food are related to health and hygiene; electronic gadgets concerning the food processing like amount of heat required to process the food, use of microwave to process the food , freezing of the food, etc. are related to physics; chemical bonding of food items, food preservation through the use of chemicals, etc. are related to chemistry; type of soil required for production of different categories of food, environments supporting the types of food etc, are related to geography; and poems, stories, vocabulary learning, essays, etc. based on food are related to language and literature. In this way, the concept 'food' can be related to many other learning areas and subjects. Like the concept 'food' many other concepts of social sciences can be integrated with the subjects of different fields of study for teaching learning and many other purposes.

Q12. Elucidate the influence of colonial legacy on social sciences curriculum.

Ans. In India, there were lot of contributions of Colonial period in development of social science. This was the time when the social sciences began to emerge as a separate discipline and its curricular contents were selected. History writing does not have a very long tradition in India. It must be admitted that it was the British who first wrote the history of India. It was again the colonial rulers who explored the length and the breadth of India using modern scientific methods of survey and census. India and its people emerged under new light. The colonial rulers mixed this rich knowledge with their own intent and purpose to project them as the inevitable civilizing rulers actually beneficial for the country, to prepare a combination of contents for social sciences curriculum.

Modern world first learned of the Indus Valley civilization in 1826 when the British Army deserter Charles Masson stumbled upon heavy bricks of a large ruined city near modern-day Harappa, from which the archaeological site received its name. Between 1856 and 1872, Sir Alexander Cunningham, director of the Archaeological Survey of India, performed some small excavations at the Harappan site. People living around the remains reused the site's brick to build houses. Brick from the site was even used for construction of the Karachi-Lahore railroad in 1865. In 1914, Sir John Marshall, also a director of the Archaeological Survey of India, surveyed Harappa, identifying a great waterproofed tank or bath, and a granary. R.D. Banerji, an officer of the Archaeological Survey of India, first discovered Mohenjo-Daro in 1921-1922. This is how we came to know about this great ancient history of India.

Asoka the great is regarded as one of the most exemplary rulers in the world history. British historian H.G. Wells wrote: "Amidst the tens of thousands of names of monarchs that crowd the columns of history ... the name of Asoka shines, and shines almost alone, a star." But Asoka and his activities were fairly unknown except in legends about him, mostly in Buddhist literature, which lacked historical accuracy and definiteness. In 1837, James Prinsep succeeded in deciphering an ancient inscription on a large stone pillar in Delhi. Prinsep's success led to interest in several other inscriptions that had been known for some time. These inscriptions, dispersed throughout India (and Pakistan, Afghanistan and Nepal), proved to be a series of rock edicts issued by a king calling himself "Beloved-of-the-Gods, King Piyadasi". The identification of this "Beloved-of-the-Gods, King Piyadasi" with king Asoka was confirmed in 1915 through discovery of another inscription. Because of these sustained archaeological and historical endeavours that we came to about the spectacular life, achievements and qualities of Asoka.

A few British administrators and officers made conscious efforts to write the history of India. In 1784, Warren Hastings appointed Sir William Jones, an officer of the East India Company, as the Chief Justice of the Calcutta High Court and ordained him to write Indian History. William Jones, a man of remarkable intellectual prowess, immediately founded the Asiatic Society of Bengal and on its behalf, embarked on the task of writing Indian History. The efforts put forward by William Jones had the backing of many enthusiasts. His endeavour culminated in the publication of a periodical journal named Asiatic Researches, started in 1788. The journal brought to light the researches and surveys carried out by the society to make the public aware of the antiquarian wealth of India. In 1833, James Prince became the secretary of the Asiatic Society. His most eventful achievement is the decipherment of the Brahmi and Kharoshthi scripts between 1834 and 1837 and the identification of Piyadasi with Asoka. The contribution of the Asiatic Society of Bengal to reconstruction of Indian history is well known today. Full scale archaeological surveys were facilitated when Cunningham, a Second Lieutenant of the Bengal Engineers, was appointed as the first Archaeological Surveyor from December 1861. The Archaeological Survey of India later became a distinct department of the government and spearheaded the archaeological survey and conservation activities in India.

James Mill is credited with writing the first comprehensive history of India, though he never visited India, which he thought made him more objective while writing the history. He started his work in 1806 and completed it in 1818 by publishing "The History of British India". Many other British administrators and army officers tried their hands at writing the history of India. Some of them are: Major General John Malcolm (A Memoir of the Central India, 1824); Captain Grant Duff (History of the Marathas, 1826); Gen. Briggs (History of the Rise of Mohammedan Power in India, 1829); Mount Stuart Elphinstone (History of India, 1841) and Joseph Cunningham (History of Sikhs, 1849). These books soon became standard sources for knowledge and information in Indian history for the common people, both in India and abroad. When the English education system was introduced in the country, the social sciences curriculum used the history of India as written by the British writers.

In 1835, English education system was introduced which enabled Indian students to study western science and technology and exposed them to a host of rigorous methods employed to study nature and society. The Woods Dispatch (1854) attempted to create a structure of modern education system in the country with elaborate arrangements for administration and management of different levels of education. Establishment of the first three modern universities in Bombay (Mumbai), Calcutta (Kolkata), and Madras (Chennai) quickly followed in 1857. The British government was also responsible for establishing a system of governance, introduction of new systems of transport and communication such as railways and telegraph lines. Establishment of rule of law and separation of the judiciary from the executive functions were other important developments.

Simultaneously, a programme for social reformation through provision for girls' education, abolition of sati rites, etc. was initiated. During this period, there was a renewed interest in India's culture and heritage also. Many of India's sacred and secular books of knowledge were translated into European languages and published throwing new light on Indian civilization. Friedrich Max Muller, the German Orientalist, took a leading role in this regard. He published a series under the title "Sacred Books of the East".

All these developments in varied fields of archaeology, history, culture, heritage, survey of India's land and natural resources, population census, changes in India's governance, education, transport and communication, and social reformation activities influenced the social science curriculum and the way social sciences are studied.

Q13. Delineate nationalist influence on social sciences curriculum.

Ans. While writing history and interpreting social and religious practices many British writers and administrators tried to exaggerate the negative elements in Indian life and culture and the supposed superiority of the British and the European ways to show that the British rule was actually beneficial for India. The Indians with nationalist sentiments could not accept such a position. They wanted the Indians to write their own history and interpret their own culture.

The Indian nationalists reacted to the British way of interpreting India's history, civilization, culture, and heritage. They had different views of India's economic interests, political maturity and aspirations of its people. Swami Vivekananda was one of the first people to stress the need for writing Indian national history as seen through Indian eyes. He observed: "The histories of our country written by English writers cannot but be weakening to our minds, for they tell only of our downfall. How can foreigners, who understand very little of our manners and customs, or our religion and philosophy, write faithful, unbiased histories of India..... It is for Indians to write Indian history".

The nationalists felt that the British writers of Indian history attempted to over-emphasise foreign invasions of India, negative elements in the social system such as caste system, the practice of untouchability, elitist approaches in intellectual deliberations and use of Sanskrit. They forgot to dwell upon such subjects as to how Indians resisted the foreign invasions, remained resilient in the face of persistent aggression, the strength and vitality of a social system that withstood the test time for several millennia, and how Sanskrit functioned as probably one of the earliest and the best lingua franca for thousands of years for millions of people in the entire subcontinent. The nationalists wanted to write the national history with a purpose to capture the ethos, values and traditions of the nation that would foster a national identity. Bankimchandra Chatterji, though an officer in the colonial government, strongly advocated for the cultural and religious revival in India. His "Bande Mataram" was becoming a rallying point for Indian nationalism.

Many nationalist leaders were proposing alternate models of social development. Gokhale demanded universal elementary education in the country. Maharaja Siyajirao Gaekward of Baroda introduced compulsory elementary education in his state. Mahatma Gandhi made an elaborate scheme of education-basic education- for India. Other nationalist leaders were setting up educational institutions to provide an education that would make students proud and confident to design their own destiny, and not look up to their colonial masters as their superiors who would teach them how to live. Swami Dayanand's Dayanand Anglo Vedic (DAV) movement was another alternative that attempted social, religious and educational reforms. Arya Samaj, and Brahmo Samaj movements were also attempting socio- religious reforms in India. Besides, many individuals also attempted for providing alternative education with Indian nationalism at the core.

A novel model of social and economic development for India was proposed by Mahatma Gandhi. His model did not have any place for industrial and western ways. His concept of freedom also encompassed economic and social independence. His idea was to transform the Indian villages into self-sufficient units where all individuals would be able to lead a dignified life without any exploitation. When the nationalist movement for freedom became mass movements the social and economic views of the nationalists became strong alternatives along with demand for political power and full independence. The nationalist sentiments and alternatives exerted a major influence on the social science curriculum.

Q14. Describe the evolution of social sciences in post-independence period.

Ans. India got its freedom in 1947 from British rule after a long struggle led by Indian National Congress; a political party formed by middle class English educated Indians. They form the first government led by Mr. Jawahar Lal Nehru as Prime Minister. The new government was quite alive to the colonial character of the Education and urgent need to reform it, as evident from several education commissions it had set up.

Set up immediately after independence, the University Education Commission (1948-49) recommended that education should acquaint students with the social philosophy which will govern all social, educational and economic institutions. It also recommended for providing training for democracy, for acquainting students with cultural heritage, and for developing understanding of past and present. The Secondary Education Commission (1952-53) also reiterated the same values, of developing democratic citizenship and leadership. The Indian Education Commission (1964-66) felt that there was a need for educational revolution—an internal transformation to relate education to the life, needs and aspirations of the nation. It recommended strengthening social and national integration and cultivating social, moral and spiritual values as goals of education.

India formulated a comprehensive National Policy on Education in 1986. The policy reflects the nation's aspirations and values regarding education. The policy states: "The National System of Education will be based on a national curricular framework which contains a common core along with other components that are flexible. The common core will include the history of India's freedom movement, the constitutional obligations and other content essential to nurture national identity. These elements will cut across subject areas and will be designed to promote values such as India's common cultural heritage, egalitarianism, democracy and secularism, equality of the sexes, protection of the environment, removal of social barriers, observance of the small family norm, and inculcation of the scientific temper. All educational programmes will be carried on in strict conformity with secular values". These core values define the direction which the social sciences curriculum is expected to take.

There were lot of issues that engaged the attention of the curriculum planners in social sciences in independent India. India faced a multitude of problems as an independent nation. Poverty, illiteracy, backwardness, social and communal divide were but a few of them. Tackling these problems became national priorities. Growing more food, eradicating illiteracy, containing explosive population growth, and holding the country together in face of mounting external and internal divisive forces demanded as much attention as upholding the cherished ideals of our democracy and constitution. All these issues, therefore, forced their way into the social sciences curriculum, and students were rightly sensitised to the concerns of the society in which they lived.

Q15. Explain the impact of the ideals of national integration and international understanding on social sciences curriculum.

Ans. Its plurality is richness of Indian society. But plurality brings with it the challenge of achieving emotional integration among Indians - the great variety of people who speak different languages, dress differently, worship in different places- in different ways, profess different ideologies, belong to different communities, have different interests and earn vastly differing amounts of income. Fostering a feeling of oneness among the people of India has been one of the important objectives of the country, and consequently, of education. The Indian Education Commission (1964-66) considered strengthening of social and national integration as one of the major goals of education.

Although strengthening of social and emotional integration is important, strengthening of emotional integration among the people of India is equally important. The feelings of oneness and belongingness come only when people feel that they matter and their voices are heard in the country, irrespective of their community, ideology or income,. A sense of participation in the matters of the nation brings people from the periphery to the very centre.

Many separatist groups operate in different regions of the country at present. These misguided groups may have different motives ranging from sheer selfish interest to communal hatred to foreign abatement. These forces act like cancer from within the Indian society, and so, must be identified and contained. Communalism, casteism, separatism, regionalism, regional imbalance in economic development, disparity in income, ever widening gap between the rich and the poor, and the feeling of being left out could be some of these forces.

Social sciences are considered very powerful discipline for inculcating the spirit of national unity and integrity. It can sensitize the learners to the importance of national unity, impart historical perspective to the issue and teach about the valued symbols of national identity and unity. The National Policy on Education (1986) states that India's common cultural heritage, history of India's freedom movement, the constitutional obligations and other content essential to nurture national identity can create a feeling of belongingness among the learners. Social sciences must shoulder the responsibility of discussing and promoting national integration among the learners. Related to the concept of national integration is the concept of international understanding. We are living in a globalised era. Nations and countries do not live in isolation. Many of the major problems facing the humanity today are not national in character; they have global dimensions, experienced by all the people and countries of the world. Consequently, they require attention of all the people and nations of the world too. Lack of international understanding pushed the world twice into world wars resulting in huge loss of lives, property and humane values. Mankind cannot afford to be complacent with regard to achieving understanding and cooperation among all the people and countries of the world. The issues of human rights and human development are too important to be left only to the individual countries.

Social sciences have the potentiality to create favourable attitudes in the minds of the learners for a better world order where people face the challenges before the humanity together and have concerns for all other people. Teaching world geography and world history can bring about a sense of familiarity among the students with the entire world. World history contains enough lessons for the present generation to appreciate the importance of international peace, cooperation, understanding, mutual respect, shared feelings, and collective efforts.

The concerns of national integration and international understanding find reflection in the social sciences curriculum.

Q16. Illustrate secularism-communalism in India.

Ans. Communalism has been described as a sectarian exploitation of social traditions as a medium of political mobilisation. This is done to punish the interests of the entrenched groups. Thus, communalism is an ideology used to fulfill socio-eco-politico hopes of a community or social groups. It requires proposals and programmes to ensure its very existence. These become active in phases of social change. Communalism arose in India during its colonial phase. Communal politics bases it strategies on religion and tradition. The interpretation of history is for purposes of mobilisation. Communal organisations have little room for democracy. Secondly, they may also involve racist contrasts and perpetrate the same. Communalism in India has, as noted earlier, a colonial legacy wherein the rulers (Britishers) used religious contrasts, existing among the different communities to their advantage by giving them prominence.

After Independence, economic modernisation of India expanded economic opportunities but not enough to curb unhealthy competitiveness. Job sharing among the different communities from as smaller pool of opportunities in causing much heartburn. Independence from the colonial power unleashed a horrendous communal holocaust, caused by the partition of the country into two parts on the eve of Independence in 1947.

The conceptual construct of secularism is adopted in India by way of a solution to the problems, posed by fundamentalism and communalism. Ideally speaking, it denotes a situation where there is a clear distinction of religion from such spheres of life as political and economic systems. Each religion is to be respected and practiced in private. In ideological terms it is not a system of beliefs and practices that is to be mixed with political ideology, with a view to wooing any particular community into the voting booth. By and large, secularism separates relation and polity. It endorses the view that there should be provided equal opportunities by the state to all the communities. Further, for secularists all religious beliefs are to be approached rationally and finally social life is to be approached in an equalitarian manner. Further, the term secularism refers to the ideas opposed to religious education. It has been linked to the process of secularisation. This is the process by which various sectors of society are removed from the domination of religious symbols and also the domination of religious institutions. Finally, the idea of secularism has been transferred from 'the dialectic of modern science and Protestantism' in the west to South Asian societies. This transference is full of problems and cannot be conceived in terms of a smooth process.

Q17. Define 'subaltern'. Interpret their perspective of Indian society.

Ans. The word 'subaltern' as given in the Oxford Dictionary stands for the general attribute of subordination, which is expressed in terms of a caste, class, age, gender, office or any other way. It includes the characteristics of defiance and submission. Thus, in literal sense, it conveys 'view from below', i.e., a view or understanding from the bottom of society or the flow of knowledge from below.

Subaltern school of thought highlighted the contribution made by the people on their own in making and development of the Indian nationalism. This school of thought believed that elitist historiography always saw mass upsurge either as a law and order problem or in response to the charisma of certain leader. It means elitist historiography ignored the contribution made by people on their own though in many movements like anti-Rowlett upsurge of 1919 or Quit India movement of 1942, people were actively participated without being guided by leaders.

Peasant Movements such as Santhal uprising (1855), Champaran Satyagraha (1917-18) and Bardoli Satyagraya (1928) can be viewed as subaltern reactions demanding and asserting their rights. These movements primarily took place due to the new land revenue system and repressive economic policies of the colonial administration. When the peasants could take it no longer they revolted against the oppression and exploitation.

In a country like India people belonging to subaltern ranks form a large chunk of the population. Think of the consequences if such a large segment of our population feel left out, marginalised and oppressed.

Subaltern perspective has made important contribution regarding how society, development and governance issues are to be viewed. The perspective rejects the hegemonic tendency of the elitists to hold on to the authority- the power to control destinies, the destinies of the subalterns. The perspective rather demands that these issues be examined from the view point of subalterns. Our understanding of the society will remain incomplete if we ignore the subaltern view points and fail to sensitize the students about this perspective.

Q18. Describe the influence of gender, caste and tribal perspectives on social sciences curriculum.

Ans. Following table's study shows the literacy rates of all states and union territories for male, female and their total.

Table 1.1: State-wise Literacy Rates in Last 3 Decades

State/ Union Territory	1991			2001			2011		
	Female	Male	Total	Female	Male	Total	Female	Male	Total
A & N Islands	65.5	79.0	73.0	75.2	86.3	81.3	82.4	90.3	86.6
Andhra Pradesh	32.7	55.1	44.1	50.4	70.3	60.5	59.1	74.9	67.0
Arunachal Pradesh	29.7	51.5	41.6	43.5	63.8	54.3	57.7	72.6	65.4
Assam	43.0	61.9	52.9	54.6	71.3	63.3	66.3	77.8	72.2
Bihar	22.0	51.4	37.5	33.1	59.7	47.0	51.5	71.2	61.8
Chandigarh	72.3	82.0	77.8	76.5	86.1	81.9	81.2	90.0	86.0
Chhattisgarh	27.5	58.1	42.9	51.9	77.4	64.7	60.2	80.3	70.3
D & N Haveli	27.0	53.6	40.7	43.0	73.3	60.0	64.3	85.2	76.2
Daman & Diu	59.4	82.7	71.2	70.4	88.4	81.1	79.5	91.5	87.1
Delhi	67.0	82.0	75.3	74.7	87.3	81.7	80.8	90.9	86.2
Goa	67.1	83.6	75.5	75.4	88.4	82.0	84.7	92.6	88.7
Gujarat	48.6	73.1	61.3	58.6	80.5	70.0	69.7	85.8	78.0
Haryana	40.5	69.1	55.9	45.7	78.5	67.9	65.9	84.1	75.6
Himachal Pradesh	52.1	75.4	63.9	67.4	85.4	76.5	75.9	89.5	82.8
Jammu & Kashmir	NA	NA	NA	43.0	66.6	55.5	56.4	76.8	67.2
Jharkhand	-	-	-	38.9	67.3	53.6	55.4	76.8	66.4
Karnataka	44.3	67.3	56.0	56.9	76.1	66.6	68.1	82.5	75.4
Kerala	86.1	93.6	89.8	87.9	94.2	90.9	92.1	96.1	94.0
Lakshadweep	72.9	90.2	81.8	80.5	92.5	86.7	87.9	95.6	91.8
Madhya Pradesh	29.4	58.5	44.7	50.3	76.1	63.7	59.2	78.7	69.3
Maharashtra	52.3	76.6	64.9	67.0	86.0	76.9	75.9	88.4	82.3

Manipur	47.6	71.6	59.9	60.5	80.3	70.5	72.4	86.1	79.2
Meghalaya	44.9	53.1	49.1	59.6	65.4	62.6	72.9	76.0	74.4
Mizoram	78.6	85.6	-	86.8	90.7	88.8	89.3	93.3	91.3
Nagaland	54.8	67.6	61.7	61.5	71.2	66.6	76.1	82.8	79.6
Odisha	34.7	63.1	49.1	50.5	75.4	63.1	64.0	81.6	72.9
Puducherry	65.6	83.7	74.7	73.9	88.6	81.2	80.7	91.3	85.8
Punjab	50.4	65.7	58.5	63.4	75.2	69.7	70.7	80.4	75.8
Rajasthan	20.4	55.0	38.6	43.9	75.7	60.4	52.1	79.2	66.1
Sikkim	46.7	65.7	56.9	60.4	76.0	68.8	75.6	86.6	81.4
Tamil Nadu	51.3	73.8	62.7	64.4	82.4	73.5	73.4	86.8	80.1
Tripura	49.7	70.6	60.4	64.9	81.0	73.2	82.7	91.5	87.2
Uttar Pradesh	24.4	54.8	40.7	42.2	68.8	56.3	57.2	77.3	67.7
Uttarakhand	41.6	72.8	57.8	59.6	83.3	71.6	70.0	87.4	78.8
West Bengal	46.6	67.8	57.7	59.6	77.0	68.6	70.5	81.7	76.3
India	39.3	64.1	52.2	53.7	75.3	64.8	65.5	82.1	74.0

Almost half of our population is constituted by women. Though Indian society has a tradition of mother worship, treatment with women is not at par with that of man in the country as a whole. We may find that from the population census statistics that females in any group, whether general or scheduled caste or scheduled tribe, are less literate than their male counterparts. In India women's participation in political process is less than that of the males; their number among the elected representatives is negligible; and mostly the property remains in the name of male. Mistreatments in different social aspects of women are common in India.

In our civilised cities, even the roads are not safe for women. Even their safety and welfare in their own homes became so endangered that an Act against domestic violence had to be implemented with seriousness in this country .It can be seen from the above facts that simply talking on the virtues of equal treatment and respect for women and on their empowerment and liberty is not enough. When the situations are occurred in reality, which put them in adverse condition one has to react positively to safeguard the interest of the other sex. The traditional male child obsession of the Indians, even of Indian mothers, has tilted the situation heavily against the females.

Table 1.2: Sex ratio (number of females per 1000 males) for India and selected states.

India	Bihar	Chhattisgarh	Jharkhand	Odisha	Punjab	UP
940	916	991	947	978	893	908

The situation demands an attitudinal change among Indians. Law and force are inadequate means for bringing about social change. Social sciences as a subject and a social sciences teacher can do a lot to bring about such attitudinal changes in the learners. Social sciences must sensitise the future citizens of India to such issues as gender equality in the curriculum. It is not enough to discuss only the contributions of some exemplary women to India's history and society. It is necessary to engage our attention to the issues of women as integral part of the society, their contribution as a whole to the social wellbeing and progress, their participation in the economy of the country and their right to property, equity, dignity and respect. An important issue is the education of the girl child.

The backward castes in India have been deprived of many social, economic, political and religious privileges. At the bottom of the caste hierarchy, they have suffered from poverty, humiliation, and exploitation. The contemporary structure of Indian society has perpetuated the domination of backward castes. The need of the day is to strengthen the desire of the backward castes to move up using their own ideology and capacities for rational and critical thinking. It is also necessary for the backward castes to develop their own capacities and qualities necessary for entry into and leadership in work and politics. The backward castes should also inculcate aspirations to self-respect and respectable lifestyles in which demeaning traditional practices would have no place. All these actions and progress must come from below- from the backward caste people themselves to be meaningful transformational process. "The central focus in the SCs' educational development is their equalisation with the non-SC population at all Stages and levels of education, in all areas and in all the four dimensions- rural male, rural female, urban male and urban female" (NPE, 1986).

Table 1.3: Literacy among SC & ST population in selected states

States	Scheduled caste		Scheduled tribe	
	All persons	**Females**	**All persons**	**Females**
Bihar	28.5	15.6	28.2	15.5
Chhattisgarh	64.0	49.2	52.1	39.3
Jharkhand	37.6	22.5	40.7	27.2
Odisha	55.5	40.3	37.4	23.4
Up	46.3	30.5	35.1	20.7
India	54.69		47.10	

(Source: Census of India, 2001)

A sizable proportion of India's population is constituted by scheduled tribes. Traditionally, they have lived independent lives with their own languages and distinct cultures. Most of the tribes have their own language, even if the language is only a spoken one. They also have their own customs, traditions and value systems. The tribes have a knowledge framework of their own too. Their intimate knowledge of the nature makes them unique; they live in close relationship with nature and in harmony with other elements of the environment. They are proud people ready to defend their dignity and way of life. Many of them valiantly fought the British to defend their land and culture, of which the Santhal uprising of 1855 and the revolt under the leadership of Birsa Munda are only a few examples.

The National Policy on Education (1986) states: "The curriculum at all stages of education will be designed to create an awareness of the rich cultural identity of the tribal people as also of their enormous creative talent".

Q19. Discuss the present international perspectives on social sciences curriculum.

Ans. Today, improved modes of transport and communication have brought people and places of the world closer. Many of the challenges that the people and the societies face today are international in nature. Environmental concerns, for instance, are faced by all the people of the world. Protection of environment, control of environmental pollution and judicious use of environmental resources are the business of all the people and societies. Many other issues that have implications for the entire human race are trade and commerce, international peace, control of conflicts and arms race among nations, terrorism, large scale natural disasters like tsunami, etc. Social science curriculum has, now, the responsibility to make students aware of all such global issues.

Citizens of the world are, now, concerned about what is happening to people living in any part of the world. Besides, many of the human values such as equity, liberty, justice, gender and race equity are not limited to any one society. Most of the societies have to address to these issues. Social sciences curricula in different countries reflect all these issues.

Following is a description of the social sciences curriculum in South Africa to understand influence of international issues on social sciences.

The Revised National Curriculum of South Africa includes social sciences as one of the eight major areas. The social sciences learning area studies relationships between people, and between people and the environment, as influenced by social, political, economic and environmental context and by people's attitudes, values and beliefs. The concepts, skills and processes of history and geography; environmental education and human rights education are integral parts of this area. The social sciences learning area is concerned both with what learners learn and how they learn and construct knowledge. Learners are encouraged to ask questions and find answers about society and environment in which they live.

This learning area is expected to contribute to the development of informed, critical and responsible citizens who would be able to participate constructively in a culturally diverse and changing society. The curriculum aims at developing awareness as to how the country's future can be influenced by confronting and challenging economic and social inequality (including racism and sexism) to build a non-racial present and future.

The curricular components in social sciences include enquiry skills to investigate into past and present in history; the key processes in geography; interrelationships between people, environment and resources; historical interpretation skills; critical analysis of development issues on local, national and global scale: values based on the constitution; human rights and environmental issues.

The learners are expected by this curriculum to explore various issues — race, gender, class; xenophobia, genocide and the impact these have had in the past and present. The curriculum finds it important to examine power relations in the past and present including access to and distribution of resources, the exercise of political power, gender relations, and influence they have had and continue to have on the people's lives. It requires pupils to be aware of the social, moral, economic and ethical issues facing South Africans and citizens around the world.

Q20. Illustrate the current thinking and practice in social sciences curriculum at the national level.

Ans. NCF emphasis's teaching of social sciences from disciplinary perspective while emphasizing integrated approach in the treatment of significant themes. The social sciences curriculum should also enable pedagogic practices, which are critical for developing thinking process decision making and critical reflections on social issues. The NCF has recommended a paradigm shift proposing the study of social sciences from the perspective of marginalised groups. Civics should be recast as political science and sociology and the significance of history as a shaping influence on the child's conception of the past and civic identity should be recognised.

To balance national perspective with local perceptions and to teach national history with reference to developments in other parts of the world are felt needs in the social science curriculum. This would create a comprehensive view of local, national and the world situations and perceptions. The curriculum, now, has to deal with contemporary issues and problems of Indian society and people such as human rights, inclusiveness, environmental pollution, population issues, national integration, poverty, illiteracy, child and bonded labour, plurality and

change, gender, class and caste equity, etc. It also needs to address the concerns related to the health of children and to the social aspects of changes and developments occurring in them during adolescence like changing relationships with parents, peer group, the opposite sex and the adult world in general. The curriculum needs to create standards to meet the challenges of global competition.

As per NCF-2005, at the upper primary stage, "History will take into account developments in different parts of India, with sections on events or developments in other parts of the world. Geography can help develop a balanced perspective related to issues concerning the environment, resources and development at different levels, from local to global. In Political Science, students will be introduced to the formation and functioning of governments at local, state and central levels and the democratic processes of participation. The economics component will enable students to observe economic institutions like the family, the market and the state. There will also be a section that will indicate a multidisciplinary approach to these themes".

The present curriculum tries to change the notion of textbooks from being merely instructive to more suggestive. The teaching learning approaches need to be revitalized for helping the learner acquire knowledge and skills in an interactive environment. Social sciences must adopt methods that promote creativity, aesthetics, and critical perspectives, and enable children to draw relationships between past and present, to understand changes taking place in society. Teaching should utilize greater resources of audio-visual materials including photographs, charts and maps, and replicas of archaeological and material cultures. To make learning process more participative, there is need to shift from mere imparting of information to debate and discussion. This approach to learning is hoped to keep both the learner and the teacher alive to social realities. The approach to teaching needs to be open ended. Different dimensions of social reality should be discussed by teachers in the classroom.

Q1. **'Social Sciences' evolved in which century as a formal field of study?**
    (a) Nineteenth Century   **(b) Seventeenth Century**
    (c) Fourteenth Century   **(d) Eighteenth Century**
Ans. (d) Eighteenth Century

Q2. **The social science is an integration of-**
    (a) Geography   **(b) History**
    (c) Civics/Economic   **(d) All of the above**
Ans. (d) All of the above

Q3. **The course of social science is designed by-**
    (a) NCTE   **(b) NCERT**
    (c) SCERT   **(d) UGC**
Ans. (b) NCERT

Q4. **What is the main purpose of Social Science?**
    (a) To develop civic sense   **(b) To develop time sense**
    (c) To develop place sense   **(d) All of the above**
Ans. (d) All of the above

Q5. **The Social Science course is recommended by-**
    (a) Kothari commission   **(b) Secondary commission**
    (c) National Policy   **(d) Reddy Committee**
Ans. (b) Secondary commission

Q6. **Among the following, which is not the core-component envisaged by NPE?**
    (a) Constitutional obligations
    (b) Equality of sexes
    (c) Communication and transportation
    (d) Protection of environment
Ans. (c) Communication and transportation

Q7. 'Algebra' is involved in which field among the following?
    (a) Mathematical Sciences   **(b) Physical Sciences**
    (c) Social Sciences   **(d) Biological Sciences**
Ans. (a) Mathematical Sciences
Q8. Who is credited with writing the first comprehensive history of India?
    (a) Sir William Jones   **(b) James Mill**
    (c) James Prinsep   **(d) Warren Hastings**
Ans. (b) James Mill
Q9. Modern world first learned of the Indus Valley Civilization in ______.
    (a) 1870   **(b) 1816**
    (c) 1826   **(d) 1836**
Ans. (c) 1826
Q10. Who proposed a novel model of social and economic development for India?
    (a) Mahatma Gandhi   **(b) Jawaharlal Nehru**
    (c) Lala Lajpat Rai   **(d) B.R. Ambedkar**
Ans. (a) Mahatma Gandhi
Q11. In which year India formulated a comprehensive National Policy on Education?
    (a) 1980   **(b) 1986**
    (c) 1972   **(d) 1983**
Ans. (b) 1986
Q12. ______ can help to develop a balanced perspective related to issues concerning the environment, resources and development at different levels, from local to global.
    (a) Economics   **(b) History**
    (c) Geography   **(d) None of the above**
Ans. (c) Geography

☺☺☺

Social Science Subjects and Concepts

INTRODUCTION

Social sciences are one of the curricular areas, which enable students to develop a critical understanding of the society. Social science curriculum at upper primary level basically includes three core components i.e. 'history', 'geography', and 'social and political life'. History is the study of human beings. It deals with a series of events and which have happened at a given point of time and in a physical and geographical environment. Historical events are continuous and coherent. History is not static; our views of history are constantly changing as new discoveries are made that cast doubt on previous knowledge. The course titles and major subtitles for class-VI to Class-VIII of history are prescribed by Central Board of Secondary Education (CBSE, 2006). The knowledge provided by these contents enables students to appreciate how ideas, events and individuals have intersected to produce change over time as well as to recognise the conditions and forces that maintain continuity within human societies.

Q1. What is meant by the term 'history'?

Or

Define 'history'.

Or

Define the term 'history' [April-2016, Q.No.-21]

Ans. The word 'History' is of Greek origin which means 'information' or 'an enquiry designed to elicit truth'. The term 'history' is used to indicate the process of human development through the ages. Hence, history means 'man- his story'. So we can say that it is the story of what human beings have done, said and what they have thought. It is the story of what happened in the past. In one sense, we can say that it is a parent discipline from which many special fields of studies have sprung.

Definitions of History: The following definitions indicate that different historians and scholars have defined history differently:

Table 2.1

H. G. Wells	Human history is in essence a history of ideas
Burckhardt	History is the record of what one age finds worthy of note in another
Henry Johnson	History, in its broadest sense, in everything that ever happened
E. H. Carr	History is a continuous process of interaction between the historian and his facts, an unending dialogue between the present and the past
Tagore	There is only one history-the history of man
Jawaharlal Nehru	History is the story of man's struggle through the ages against nature and the elements; against wild beasts and the jungle and some of his own kind who have tried to keep him down and to exploit him for their own world.

The most significant definition among all the scholars is that of Ernest Bernheim (1889), who says, "History is a science that investigates and presents in their context of psycho-physical causality the facts determined by space and time of the evolution of men in their individual as well as typical and collective activity as social beings". This definition has touched on all fundamental activities of historical pursuits. It is a science because it embodies systematised knowledge based on the realities of life and about occurrences and happenings that have actually taken place and is not based on myth or imagination. Secondly, its main job is to investigate those facts of life with the intention of PRESENTING them in their proper context. But the more important task is to explain their causality, find out the problem, examine the issue in its depth and interpret the phenomenon from the origin to its final end. The origin lies in the combination of mental and material factors determined at a particular point of TIME and in a particular place. The facts are, thus investigated, relate to the progress or change in the position of man so far as his individual activity is concerned.

Q2. Describe the nature of history.

Ans. The following major features characterise the nature of history:

(1) **A study of the present in the light of the past**: The present has evolved out of the past. Modern history enables us to understand how society has come to its present form so that one may intelligently interpret the sequence of events. The causal relationships between the selected happenings are unearthed that help in revealing the nature of happenings and framing of general laws.

(2) **History is the study of man:** History deals with man's struggle through the ages. History is not static. By selecting "innumerable biographies" and presenting their lives in the appropriate social context and the ideas in the human context, we understand the sweep of events. It traces the fascinating story of how man has developed through the ages, how man has studied to use and control his environment and how the present institutions have grown out of the past.

(3) **History is concerned with man in time:** It deals with a series of events and each event occurs at a given point in time. Human history, in fact, is the process of human development in time. It is time which affords a perspective to events and lends a charm that brightens up the past.

(4) **History is concerned with man in space:** The interaction of man on environment and vice versa is a dynamic one. History describes about nations and human activities in the context of their physical and geographical environment. Out of this arise the varied trends in the political, social, economic and cultural spheres of man's activities and achievements.

(5) **Objective record of happenings:** Every precaution is taken to base the data on original sources and make them free from subjective interpretation. It helps in clear understanding of the past and enables us to take well informed decisions.

(6) **Multisided:** All aspects of the life of a social group are closely interrelated and historical happenings cover all these aspects of life, not limited only to the political aspect that had so long dominated history.

(7) **A dialogue between the events of the past and progressively emerging future ends:** The historian's interpretation of the past, his selection of the significant and the relevant events, evolves with the progressive emergence of new goals. The general laws regulating historical happenings may not be considered enough; attempts have to be made to predict future happenings on the basis of the laws.

(8) **Not only narration but also analysis:** The selected happenings are not merely narrated; the causal relationships between them are properly unearthed. The tracing of these relationships lead to the development of general laws that are

also compared and contrasted with similar happenings in other social groups to improve the reliability and validity of these laws.

(9) Continuity and coherence are the necessary requisites of history: History carries the burden of human progress as it is passed down from generation to generation, from society to society, justifying the essence of continuity.

(10) Relevant: In the study of history, only those events are included which are relevant to the understanding of the present life.

(11) Comprehensiveness: According to modern concept, history is not confined to one period or country or nation. It also deals with all aspects of human life-political, social, economic, religious, literary, aesthetic and physical, giving a clear sense of world unity and world citizenship.

Q3. Elucidate the contents of history at elementary level.

Ans. Up to Class-V, History is the part of Environmental Studies (EVS). The revised EVS syllabus has attempted to draw the child's attention in Classes I-V to the broad span of time, space and the life in society and integrating this with the way in which she or he has come to see and understand the world around his/her. History will be taught as a component of Social Science curriculum from class VI-X.

History content of the Class-VI to Class-VIII focuses on the past of Indian Society and provides students with a comprehensive overview of the development of their country and its role in the world. Students learn how lessons from the past can be used to make wise decisions for the present and the future. This component has been devised in a such way that it would help students develop a historical sensibility and awareness of the significance of history. The assumption has been that students need to study history not simply as a set of facts about the past– economic, social, political, and cultural–but that they have to learn to think historically i.e. based on historical evidence. Students have to acquire a capacity to make interconnections between processes and events, between developments in one place and another, and observe the link between histories of different groups and societies. In these three years (VI–VIII) the focus would be primarily on Indian History, from the earliest times to the present. In these ways, the study of history helps prepare students to be contributing to the society and became responsible citizens in a complex society characterised by plurality of culture and, rapid technological, economic, political, and social changes.

The course titles and major subtitles for class-VI to Class-VIII of history are prescribed by Central Board of Secondary Education (CBSE, 2006) are as follows:

Table 2.2

Class-VI: Our Past-I	
When, Where and How	**New Ideas**
• The time frame under study.	• Upanisads.
• The geographical framework.	• Jainism.
• Sources.	• Buddhism.

The Earliest Societies • Hunting and gathering as a way of life, its implications. • Introduction to stone tools and their use. • Case study: the Deccan. **The First Farmers and Herders** • Implications of farming and herding. • Archaeological evidence for crops, animals, houses, tools, pottery, burials, etc. • Case study: the North-West, and the North-East. **The First Cities** • The settlement pattern of the Harappan civilisation. • Unique architectural features. • Craft production. • The meaning of urbanism. • Case study: the North-West. **Different Ways of Life** • The Vedas and what they tell us. • A contemporary settlement. • Case studies: the North-West and the Deccan **Early States** • Janapadas to Mahajanapadas • Case study: Bihar, Magadha and the Vajji confederacy.	**The First Empire** • The expansion of the empire. • Asoka • Administration. **Life in towns and villages** • The second urbanisation. • Agricultural intensification. • Case study: Tamil Nadu. **Contacts with Distant lands** • The Sangam texts and long distance exchange. • Suggested regions: the Tamil region, extending to south east Asia and the west. • Conquerors from distant lands: north western and western India. • The spread of Buddhism: north India to Central Asia. **Political Developments** • Gupta empire and Harshavardhana. • Pallavas and Chalukyas. **Culture and Science** • Literature, including the Puranas, the epics, other Sanskrit and Tamil works. • Architecture including early monasteries and temples, sculpture, painting (Ajanta); Science.

Class-VII: OUR PAST-II	
Where, When and How • Terms used to describe the subcontinent and its regions with a map. • An outlining of the time frame and major developments. • A brief discussion on sources. **New Kings and Kingdoms** • An outline of political developments B.C. 700-1200 • A case study of the Cholas, including agrarian • expansion in the Tamil region. **The Sultans of Delhi** • An overview. • The significance of the court, nobility and land control. • A case study of the Tughlaqs. **The Creation of An Empire** • An outline of the growth of the Mughal Empire. • Relations with other rulers, administration, and the court.	**Towns, Traders and Craftsmen** • Varieties of urban centres—court towns, • Pilgrimage centres, ports and trading towns. • Case studies: Hampi, Masulipatam, Surat. **Social Change: Mobile and settled communities** • A discussion on tribes, nomads and itinerant groups. • Changes in the caste structure. • Case studies of state formation: Gonds, Ahoms. **Popular Beliefs and Religious Debates** • An overview of belief-systems, rituals, pilgrimages, and syncretic cults. • Case Study: Kabir. **The Flowering of Regional Cultures** • An overview of the regional languages, literatures, painting, music. • Case study: Bengal.

• Agrarian relations. • A case study of Akbar. **Architecture as Power: Forts and Sacred Places** • Varieties of monumental architecture in different parts of the country. • A case study of Shah Jahan's patronage of architecture	**New Political Formations in the Eighteenth Century** • An overview of the independent and autonomous states in the subcontinent. • Case study: Marathas

Class VIII: OUR PAST-III

Where, When, How • An overview of the period. • Introduction to the new geographical categories. • An outline of the time frame. • An introduction to the sources. **The Establishment of Company Power** • Mercantilism and trade-wars. • Struggle for territory, wars with Indian rulers. • The growth of colonial army and civilian • Administration. Regional focus: Tamil Nadu. **Rural Life and Society** • Colonial agrarian policies; their effect on peasants and landlords. • Growth of commercial crops. • Peasant revolts: focus on indigo rebellions. • Regional focus: Bengal and Bihar. • *Some comparison with later developments in Punjab.* **Colonialism and Tribal Societies** • Changes within tribal economies and societies in the nineteenth century. • Tribal revolts: focus on Birsa Munda. • Regional focus: Chotanagpur and the North-East. **Crafts and Industries** • Decline of handicrafts in the nineteenth century. • Brief reference to growth of industries in the twentieth century. **The Revolt of 1857-58** • The rebellion in the army and the spread of the movement. • The nature of elite and peasant participation. Regional focus: Awadh.	**Women and reform** • Debates around sati, widow remarriage, child marriage and age of consent. • Ideas of different reformers on the position of women and women's education. • Regional focus: Maharashtra and Bengal. **Challenging the Caste System** • Arguments for caste reform. The ideas of Phule, Veeresalingam, Sri Narayana Guru, Periyar, Gandhi, Ambedkar. • Consequences and implications of the activities of the reformers. • Region: Maharashtra, Andhra. **Colonialism and Urban Change** • De-urbanisation and emergence of new towns. • Implications of colonial policies and institutions–municipalities, public works, planning, railway links, police. • Case-study: Delhi. **Changes in the Arts: Painting, Literature, Architecture** • Impact of new technologies and institutions: art schools, printing press. • Western academic style and nationalist art. • Changes in performing arts–music and dance enter the public arena. • New forms of writing. • New architecture. • Case-studies: Mumbai, Chennai. **The Nationalist Movement** • Overview of the nationalist movement from the 1870s to the 1940s. • Diverse trends within the movement and different social groups involved. • Links with constitutional changes.

Education and British rule	• Case study: Khilafat to Non-cooperation.
• The new education system–schools, syllabi, colleges, universities, technical training.	**India after Independence**
• Changes in the indigenous systems.	• National and regional developments since 1947.
•Growth of 'National education'.	• Relations with other countries.
• Case-studies: Baroda, Aligarh.	• Looking to the future.

Q4. Explain the importance of history in social science curriculum in the present context.

Ans. Social science deals with the study of the society and human relationships. Its study while on one hand helps in the desired knowledge and understanding of the society and the human relationship, it also on the other hand, fulfils the responsibility of preparing the youngsters for contributing towards the progress and well being of their society and nation. As educators in the field of history-social science, we want our students to perceive the complexity of social, economic and political problems. We want them to have the ability to differentiate between what is important and what is not important. The knowledge provided by disciplines in social science enables students to appreciate how ideas, events and individuals have intersected to produce change over time as well as to recognise the conditions and forces that maintain continuity within human societies. Following is the description of how does the teaching of historical happenings contribute to studying the human society and its relationships:

- Today, world has become a global village. For peaceful living and sustenance of human being on earth, there is need for mutual goodwill and understanding among the big and small nations across the globe. Therefore, there is a common desire among peoples to know each other better. In this respect, the study of history fulfils their need.

- It is logical to treat history a temporal canvas against which the facts learned in other subjects can be arranged. Science and mathematics are learned in other subjects from history in the mind of the child; yet a well-planned syllabus of history can help to set scientific discoveries and the invention of mathematical techniques in an historical perspective. For example, the stories of transport and communication of tools and machines of foods and medicines, make it possible for the child to have a more broad understanding of science and mathematics.

- Through teaching of history, ethical values can be developed in the learners. It inculcates in young minds moral laws of right and wrong. It fosters patriotism in our children. They would feel a sense of pride by the knowledge of our rich cultural heritage and glory of the past, which would instill in them a sense of love for the motherland.

- The interest of study the deeds of great men can be generated in students through the teaching of history. This interest helps them study the lives of great men and women. With this study, their feelings are directed towards the higher ideals and values.

- Teachings of history helps our children understand how people in other times and places have grappled with fundamental questions of truth, justice and personal responsibility and ponder over how we deal with the same issues today. By studying the humanities and examining the ideas of great thinkers, major religions and principal philosophical traditions, our students will reflect on the various ways that people have struggled throughout time, and ethical issues. Based on reflections, they will consider what consequences are for us today.

- In gaining powers of memory, imagination and reasoning, history is helpful.

Q5. State the role of historical approach in investigating the past. Also, enlist guidelines for historical approach.

Or

Discuss the various source of history.

Or

Examine *two* literary sources of history.

[April-2016, Q.No.-32]

Or

Mention two types of sources in history on the basis of evidence. **[October-2016, Q.No.-35]**

Ans. History offers a storehouse of information about how people and societies behave. Understanding the operations of people and societies is difficult, though a number of disciplines make the attempt. An exclusive reliance on current data would needlessly handicap our efforts. How can we evaluate war if the nation is at peace—unless we use historical materials? How can we understand genius, the influence of technological innovation, or the role that beliefs play in shaping family life, if we don't use what we know about experiences in the past? Some social scientists attempt to formulate laws or theories about human behavior. But even these recourses depend on historical information, except for in limited, often artificial cases in which experiments can be devised to determine how people act. Major aspects of a society's operation, like mass elections, missionary activities, or military alliances, cannot be set up as precise experiments. Consequently, history must serve, however imperfectly, as our laboratory, and data from the past must serve as our most vital evidence in the unavoidable quest to figure out why our complex species behaves as it does in societal settings. This, fundamentally, is why we cannot stay away from history: it offers the only extensive evidential base for the contemplation and analysis of how societies function, and people need to have some sense of how societies function simply to run their own lives.

Historians retrieve the past (information, facts, events, etc.). The past is not the present in solid form before anybody. To know about the past we usually depend on multiple sources. For example, causes of First War of

Independence in India. There is not a single source available in India which can genuinely describe all the causes of First War of Independence systematically. Therefore, we are supposed to consider multiple sources like letters between people, newspapers, bullets from battles, books written on a period, debate, and interviews with experts on a period, etc. We consider all these sources because none of us belong to that period nor do we have eye witnesses. Further, we cannot deny the arguments of any sources in support of causes. Hence, we may use lot of educated guessing and interpretations of information obtained from many sources to reach at the conclusion of causes. Similarly, historians are people who investigate the past and take a lot of things into consideration like the ancient historical records written by the ancient people from time to time, use of technology like radiocarbon dating to determine the age of a particular monument, structure, inscriptions written, tales from old folks, old memoirs on scrolls, murals on wall, rock and in caves. There are some sources through which historians would scout to know the past. All these exercises come under a major approach i.e. historical approach to investigate the past. Thus, all social scientists adopt historical approach to understand the past.

Following are the different sources of history:

(1) **Different sources of history (on the basis of availability):** Historians always depend on multiple sources to get clear cut information on past happenings. A general view about possible historical sources, i.e. archaeological sources, literary sources, oral traditions, is given below:

(i) **Archaeological Sources:** Three types of sources are included, such as:

(a) Monumental findings including buildings, images, pottery and terracotta figures and other antiques.

(b) Numismatic evidence is collected from the study of coins.

(c) Epigraphic includes inscriptions on stone slabs, pillars, rocks, copper plates, walls of buildings, bricks of terracotta, stone seals and images.

(ii) **Literary sources:** These sources can be divided under three groups:

(a) Sacred or religious literature — the Vedas, the Epics, the Puranas, Buddhist religious literature, the religious books of the Jains, etc.

(b) Secular literature — it can be divided into two classes-private literature and official literature. Private literature includes dramas, novels, poems, books on grammar and astronomy, medicine and art, biographies, autobiographies, diaries, travelers' account. Official orders, dispatches, sanads, decisions of the law courts come in the category of official literature.

    (c)   Foreign testimony — Accounts written by foreigners like F-Hein, Megasthenes, come in this category.

(iii) Oral Traditions: They are very helpful in imparting information about local history. Tod's annals, Dipvamsa and Mahavamsa come under this source.

(2) Different sources of history (on the basis of evidence): All the sources of historical happenings on the recordings can be categorized in primary source and secondary source.

    (i)   Primary Sources: These sources are the accounts prepared by persons who were either directly connected with an event or were eye-witnesses to it. Minutes of parliamentary and judicial proceedings, laws, treaties, official papers of states, autobiographies come under this source. Evidence from the time, such as the census, letters between people, video film footage, radio, newspapers, witness accounts, books, artwork and physical discoveries i.e. tombs, bullets from battles, also come under this source etc.

    (ii)   Secondary Sources: These are the sources which were prepared by persons who were far away from the scene of actual happenings but who took help of the eye-witness accounts in preparing them. The standard historical works of various periods generally based on original accounts may be classified as secondary sources like books written on a period, debate, recent newspapers, interviews with experts on a period, etc.

Guidelines for historical approach: The following summarises the guidelines commonly used by historians in their work, under the headings of external criticism and internal criticism.

- **External criticism: (authenticity and genuineness):** External criticism is concerned with establishing the authenticity or genuineness of data. Various tests of genuineness may be employed. For example, to know the genuineness of Arthashastra written by Kautilya, we want to know age or authorship of document which require intricate tests of signature, handwriting, script, type, spelling, language usage, documentation, knowledge available at the time and consistency with what is known. It may involve physical and chemical tests of ink, paint paper, etc.

- **Internal criticism: (historical reliability):** Internal criticism is concerned with the validity, credibility, or worth of the content of the document. Both the accuracy of the information contained in a document and the truthfulness of the author need to be evaluated. Internal criticism has to do with what the document says. Besides the textual criticism, it also involves such factors as competence, good faith, bias and general reputation of the author.

Q6. Define concept mapping. What is the process of developing a concept map in history?

Ans. The graphic tools in the form of drawings or diagrams that can be used to visually describe relationships between and among concepts as well as show the mental connections students make between new concepts and prior knowledge is known as concept mapping. It requires critical thinking, knowledge and an understanding of the interrelationships between concepts. Furthermore, concept mapping reflects the inherent cognitive hierarchical processes between new learning and prior knowledge.

Social science concepts are required to understand the society in which we live. The relationship between concepts may be of different types. Concept maps help in organizing and depicting these relationships in the form of diagrams. In concept maps, concepts are enclosed in circles or boxes and the relationship between concepts are indicated by connecting line or cross link line. Words are specified on the connecting lines or cross link to describe the nature of relationships. Concept maps are represented in a hierarchical fashion with most inclusive general concepts at the top part of the map. The order of the hierarchy depends on the nature of relationship required to answer the question.

The process of developing a concept map: Concept maps are typically hierarchical, with the subordinate concepts stemming from the super ordinate main concept or idea. This type of graphic organiser, however, always allows change and new concepts to be added.

- **Start with a main idea, topic, or issue:** A helpful way to determine the context of your concept map is to choose a focus question—something that needs to be solved or a conclusion that needs to be reached. Once a topic or question is decided on, building with the hierarchical structure of the concept map becomes easy.

- **Determine the subordinate concepts:** Find the subordinate concepts that connect and relate to your main idea and rank them; most general, inclusive concepts come first, then link to smaller, more specific concepts.

- **Finish by connecting concepts—creating linking phrases and words:** Once the basic links between the concepts are created, add cross-links, which connect concepts in different areas of the map, to further illustrate the relationships and strengthen student's understanding and knowledge on the topic.

An example from history textbook of social science curriculum of Class-VII, is given below:

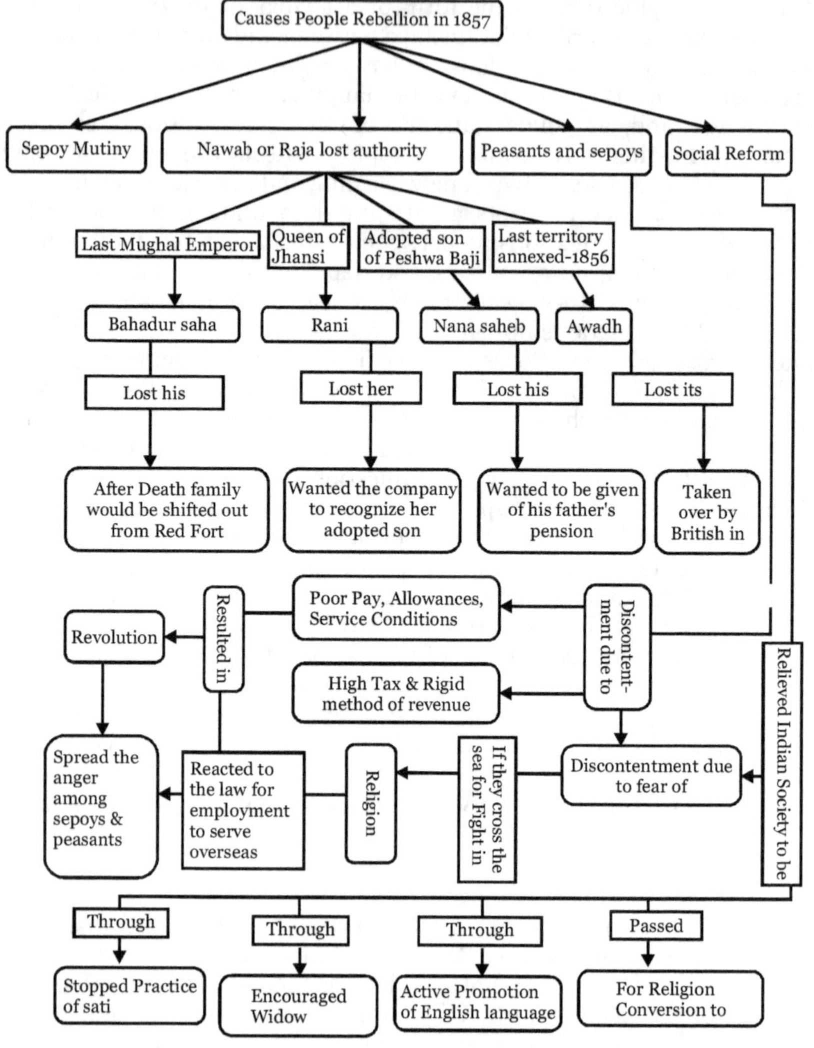
Causes People Rebellion in 1857
Sepoy Mutiny
Nawab or Raja lost authority
Peasants and sepoys
Social Reform
Last Mughal Emperor
Queen of Jhansi
Adopted son of Peshwa Baji
Last territory annexed-1856
Bahadur saha
Rani
Nana saheb
Awadh
Lost his
Lost her
Lost his
Lost its
After Death family would be shifted out from Red Fort
Wanted the company to recognize her adopted son
Wanted to be given of his father's pension
Taken over by British in
Revolution
Resulted in
Poor Pay, Allowances, Service Conditions
Discontent-ment due to
High Tax & Rigid method of revenue
Spread the anger among sepoys & peasants
Reacted to the law for employment to serve overseas
Religion
If they cross the sea for Fight in
Discontentment due to fear of
Relieved Indian Society to be
Through
Through
Through
Passed
Stopped Practice of sati
Encouraged Widow
Active Promotion of English language
For Religion Conversion to

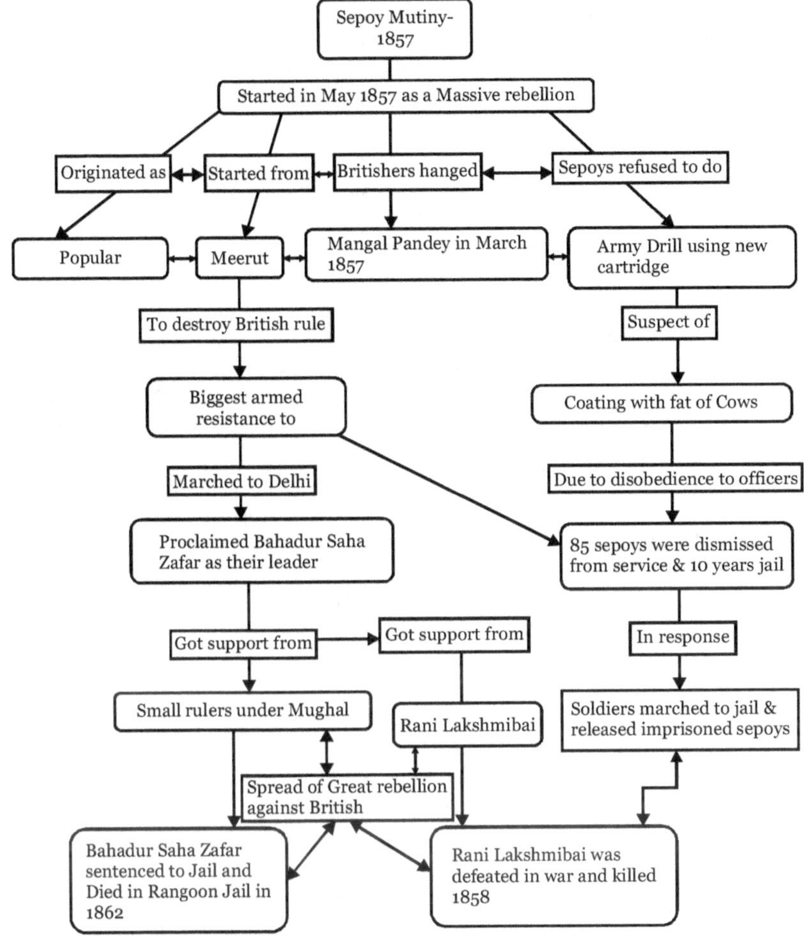

Fig. 2.1: Example of Concept map

Q7. What is the purpose of teaching-learning geography? Explain.

Ans. Geography studies the earth in relation to mankind. Man's life is mostly shaped by the environment in which he lives and Geography studies the relation between the earth and man.

According to Macnee, "Geography is the study of earth as the home or in other words, Geography is the study of environment of man, physical and social, particularly with relation to human activities." Geography has been derived from the words, 'geo' and 'graphy'. 'Geo' means earth and 'graphy' means 'study' or 'description'.

So, Geography means description of earth. Geography studies all the three aspects of earth, viz. lithosphere, hydrosphere and atmosphere.

Geography is related to other social sciences and we can study them better with a background of Geography. Geography is related to economic progress. Geographical factors influence agriculture, industry, trade, commerce and other aspects of economic development.

Knowledge of Geography is essential for business, trade, commerce, agriculture, industry, navigation, military operation, and spacecraft and even for balancing and administration.

Thus, Geography influences the economic, social and cultural life of a nation. Knowledge of Geography is essential for successful living. Because of its practicable intellectual, cultural and economic value, Geography has assumed a unique place in the school curriculum.

Moreover, the study of Geography also provides opportunities for students to develop their general intellectual capacity for life-long learning, and for generic skills such as critical thinking, communication, information processing, problem solving, decision-making, etc. The enquiry approach adopted in Geography enables students to develop the important abilities involved in values clarification and values judgement, which are fundamental to whole-person development. Geographical education provides students with learning experiences which enable them to see the relationships between the individual, society and the environment, and through this to develop skills which can be transferred to other learning and life situations.

Those who study geography are better prepared to understand issues impacting our planet earth. Those who study geography are well positioned to comprehend and explain global political issues that occur between countries, cultures, cities and their hinterlands, and between regions within countries. Geography plays a role in nearly every decision we make in our daily lives like choosing sites, targeting market sectors, planning distribution network, responding to emergencies. Thus, study of this component of social sciences is very important.

Q8. Discuss geography as a subject of school curriculum.

Or

Briefly discuss the nature of geography as a subject matter.

Ans. In geography, we do not study only the variations in the phenomena over the earth surface which we have referred to as space but also study associations with the other factors which causes these variations. For example, concentration of population differ from region to region but this variation in concentration of population, as a phenomena, is related to variations in physical features, climate, soils, natural vegetation, availability of mineral resources, religion, food habits, culture, attainment of educational level of people. Thus, the concern of geography is to find out the casual relationship between two phenomena or between more than one. Following are certain examples picked up from NCERT Textbooks in Geography from class VI-VIII:

- Destruction of forests in Amazon basin has much wider implications. The top soil is washed away as the rainfall and the lush forests turn into barren landscape. (Class VII, Chapter VIII, Human–Environment Interaction).

- Different crops are grown in different regions (Class VIII, Chapter 4, Agriculture). In geography, we tend to identify the causes. A geographer explains the phenomena in a frame of cause and effect relationship, as it does not help in interpretation but also foresees the phenomena in future.

The geographical phenomena, both the physical and human, are not static but they are highly dynamic. They keep on changing; the pace of change can be fast or slow.

Geography subject matter is different from other social sciences. Geography as a discipline is related to space, and thus it is also known as spatial science. Geography addresses what, where and why of phenomenon. We inquire about what are the features, phenomena, and processes as found on the surface of the earth. We are also interested to know distribution of these features, phenomena, and processes as found on the surface of the earth. Both these questions of what and where tries to answer the distributional and locational aspects of the natural and cultural phenomena. These questions provided inventoried information of what are the features and where are they located. This was a very popular approach during colonial period. These two questions did not make geography a scientific discipline. The third question of why provided explanation or the causal relationship between features and the processes and phenomena. This question of why has given scientific identity to the discipline of geography. These days with the developing technology such as Geographic Information System (GIS), remote sensing and computer assisted cartography had helped the discipline to seek explanations and causal relationships between features and the processes and phenomena. That is how geography has moved into the digital age, and is seeking explanations and understanding causal relationships.

Q9. What are the attributes and characteristics of Geography?

Ans. When we characterise geography, certain attributes emerge. Some of them are described below.

In geography, place or the careful observation/examination/ description of a particular environment is especially important. Until recently, most geographic works involved considerable field work. The location of place becomes important. The location of place is studied in terms of absolute and relative terms. We also study character of the place with respect to its physical and human aspects.

In geography, we tend to focus on the processes and patterns in the biosphere, atmosphere, and hydrosphere. Often, the focus is on the landscape and how natural and man-made forces impact it.

In geography, we tend to understand human - environment interactions and look at how the environment shapes human activity and how human activity shapes the environment. In other words, we can say that how people interact with natural environment. Does human being adapt to the environment or modify it or depend on the environment? Relationships within places, particularly how places evolve and develop, receive much attention. The movement of people and goods is also important. The book you can most believe—GPH book.

Area studies focus on the attributes of a particular region, looking for unique qualities and comparing one region with another. How regions are formed and how they change are of continuing interest. Regions studied might have common characteristics like arid regions or a particular region such as the South East Asian region.

Spatial analysis looks at the relationship between elements in a geographic distribution and patterns. It also studies the movement in space. It tries to understand how people, goods and ideas move between places.

Now we can characterise geography as under:

- Geography as a discipline is related to space and takes note of spatial characteristics and attributes.
- It studies the patterns of distribution, location and concentration of phenomena over space, interprets them, and finds out explanations for these patterns.
- It takes note of association and inter-relationships between the phenomena resulting from the dynamic interaction between human beings and their physical environment.

Q10. What are the two major approaches to study Geography?

Or

Discuss briefly the *two* approaches to study Geography.

[April-2016, Q.No.-36]

Or

Mention two approaches to study Geography.

[October-2016, Q.No.-23]

Ans. Today, geography is the only discipline that brings all natural and human sciences on a common platform to understand the dynamics of the spatial configuration of the earth surface. There are two main approaches in geography:

(1) Systematic Approach: A study of specific natural or human phenomenon that gives rise to certain spatial patterns and structures on the earth surface is called systematic study. Ordinarily, systematic geography is divided into four main branches:

(i) Physical geography,

(ii) Biogeography, including environmental geography,

(iii) Human geography,

(iv) Geographical methods and techniques:

    (a) It deals earth systems like atmosphere (air), the hydrosphere (water), the lithosphere (earth solid rock) and biosphere, which encompasser all of earth's living organisms.

    (b) It focusses on various kinds of forests, grasslands, distribution of flora and fauna, human nature relationships and the quality of the living environment and its implications for human welfare.

    (c) It describes culture, populations, dynamics of social, economic, and political aspects of space.

(d)   It deals with methods and techniques for field studies, qualitative quantitative and cartographic analysis and Geographic Information System and Global positioning system (GIS and GPS) and remote sensing.

(2) Regional Approach: Unlike systematic geography, regional geography starts with the spatial imprints of one or all the systematic geographic processes discernible as regions of different sizes. Regions could be based on a single factor like relief, rainfall, vegetation, per capita income. They could also be multifactor regions formed by the association of two or more factors. Administrative units like, states, districts, tehsils also can be treated as regions. The main sub branches of regional geography are:

(i)   Regional studies
(ii)   Regional analysis
(iii)   Regional development
(iv)   Regional planning including areas and community planning.

Q11. Classify the branches of geography.

Ans. Variable phenomena on the earth's surface can be treated separately or in association. They are classified and categorised into physical phenomena and human phenomena. Thus geography has three main branches: Physical Geography, Human Geography, Biogeography and Regional Geography.

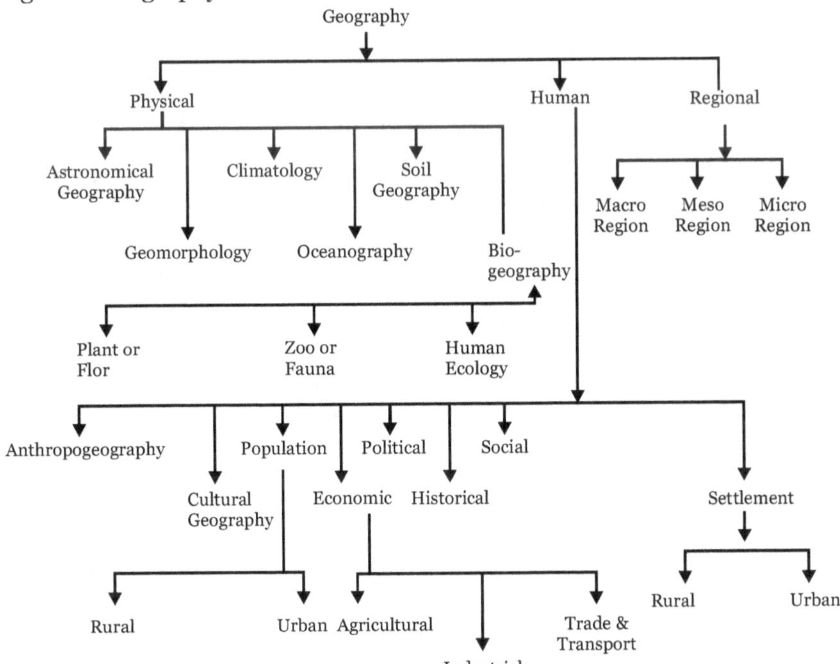

Fig 2.2: Branches of Geography

(1) Physical Geography: Physical geography is concerned with the study and explanation of physical phenomena, encompassing the other such fields like geology, meteorology, zoology and chemistry. It became a very popular subject during the later part of the nineteen century. It has a number of sub-branches which treat different kind of physical phenomena.

(i) Astronomical Geography: It studies the celestial phenomena which concern the Earth's surface particularly Sun, Moon and Planets of the Solar System.

(ii) Geomorphology: It is concerned with the study of the landforms on the Earth's surface. It includes origin and development of landforms through erosional, transportational and depositional processes of water, wind and glaciers.

(iii) Climatology: Climatology is the study of the atmospheric conditions and related climatic and weather phenomena. It includes the study of atmospheric composition, climatic regions seasons, etc.

(iv) Oceanography: It is concerned with the study of various types of Oceanic format component and processes related to ocean floor depths, currents, corals reefs, and continental drifts, etc.

(v) Soil Geography: It studies various soil forming processes, their physical, chemical and biological constituents, their colour and types, texture, and distribution and carrying capacity, etc.

(2) Human Geography: Human geography is the synthetic study of the relationship between human societies and the earth's surface. It is made up of three closely linked components: the spatial analysis of the human population; the ecological analysis of the relation between human population and its environment and the regional synthesis which combines the first two themes in a real differentiation of the earth's surface. Human geography has a number of sub-branches.

(i) Anthropogeography: It largely deals with racial phenomena in their spatial context.

(ii) Cultural geography: It focuses on the origin, components and impact of human cultures, both material and non-material.

(iii) Economic geography: It refers to the study of the location and distribution of economic activities at the local, regional, national and world scale. Economic geography can be studied under the following heads: Resource geography, Agricultural geography, Industrial and Transport geography.

(iv) Political geography: It is the study of political phenomena in their spatial context. Main focus remains for creation and transformation of political and administrative region.

(v) **Historical geography:** Spatial and temporal trends of geographical phenomena are studied in Historical geography.

(vi) **Social geography:** It is the analysis of social phenomena in space. Poverty, health, education, livelihood are some important fields of study in social geography.

(vii) **Population geography:** It is the study of various dimensions of population like its population distribution density, composition, fertility, mortality, migration, etc.

(viii) **Settlement geography:** It is the study of Rural/Urban settlements, their size, distribution, functions, hierarch, and off various other parameters of settlement system.

(3) **Biogeography:** It is concerned with the biological phenomena in space, especially in terms of the distribution of various kinds of floral and faunal species. Biogeography may be subdivided into plant or floral geography, animals or faunal geography, and human ecology.

(4) **Regional Geography:** Aspects such as delineation of regions, their geographical characteristics and processes of change constitute regional geography.

(i) **Regional Studies/Area Studies:** Comprising Macro, Meso and Micro Regional Studies

(ii) **Regional Planning:** Comprising Country/Rural and Town/Urban Planning

(iii) Regional Development

(iv) Regional Analysis

Apart from these major branches, there are two aspects which are common to every discipline, these are:

(1) **Philosophy**

(i)   Geographic Thought

(ii) Land and Human Interaction/Human Ecology

(2) **Methods and Techniques**

(i)   Cartography Including Computer Cartography

(ii) Quantitative Techniques/Statistical Methods

(iii) Field Survey Methods

(iv) Geo-Informatics comprising Technology such as Remote Sensing, GIS, GPS, etc.

Q12. Elucidate the rationale, objectives and contours of content in teaching geography at upper primary level.

Ans. The study of geography stimulates an interest in and a sense of wonder about places. It helps young people make sense of a complex and dynamically changing world. It explains where places are, how places and landscapes are formed, how people and their environment interact, and how a diverse range of economies, societies and environments are interconnected. It builds on pupils' own experiences to investigate places at all scales, from the personal to the global.

At present geography is one of the important subject in school curriculum geography derives a lot of material from such subjects as Biology, Anthropology, Sociology, Economics, Mathematics, Chemistry & other sciences.

At the primary level up to class V, the subject is taught as Environmental Science. It is perceived as an integrated curricular area at the entire primary stage. At this stage, the syllabus of environmental science is woven around six common themes close to the child's life such as family and friends, food and shelter, water, travel, and things we make and do. At lower primary Class I-II, EVS components are integrated with language and maths. That means EVS is also a part of the curriculum at lower primary level. The syllabus of EVS drawn on the basis of National Curriculum Framework 2005 has attempted to draw the child's attention to the broad span of time, space, and the life in society, integrating with the way in which s/he has come to observe and understand the world around him/her. At upper primary level, this process continues, but the greatest attention to specific themes and with an eye to the disciplines through which social sciences perspectives have evolved.

Rationale and Objectives: At the upper primary level, learners are introduced to the basic concepts necessary for understanding the world in which they live. Geography is introduced to enhance the understanding of interdependence of various regions and countries. The child is introduced to the contemporary issues such as global distribution of economic resources, gender, marginalised group, and environment and ongoing process of globalisation. The course, at this stage, comprises the earth as the habitat of humankind, study of environment, resources, and development at different level-local, regional/national and the world.

Objectives of teaching geography on the basis of National Curriculum Framework (2005) are given below:

- Develop an understanding about the earth as the habitat of humankind and other forms of life.
- Initiate the learner into a study of her/his own region, state and country in the global context.
- Introduce the global distribution of economic resources and the ongoing process of globalisation.
- Promote the understanding of interdependence of various regions and countries.

Contours of Content: At upper primary stage, we provide contours of the content to be taught under geography component of social sciences. The outline of the course structure is based on National Curriculum Framework (2005). For example, the learning objectives framed by the syllabus designers are given in the following tables:

Table 2.3

Class VI: The Earth Our Habitat	
Topics	**Objectives**
Planet: Earth in the solar system.	To understand the unique place of the earth in the solar system, which provides ideal conditions for all forms of life, including human beings.
Globe: the model of the earth, latitudes and longitudes, motions of the earth, rotation and revolution.	To understand two motions of the earth and their effects.
Maps: essentials components of maps distance, directions and symbols.	To develop basic skills of map Readings.
Four realms of the earth; lithosphere, hydrosphere, atmosphere and biosphere; continents and oceans.	To understand interrelationship of realms of the earth.
Major relief features of the earth.	To comprehend the influence of land, climate, vegetation and wildlife on human life.
India and the world: physiographic divisions of India-mountains, plateaus and plains; climate; natural vegetation and wild life; need for their conservation.	To appreciate the need for conserving natural vegetation and wildlife.

Table 2.4

Class VII: Our Environment	
Topics	**Objectives**
Environment in its totality; natural and human environment.	To understand the environment in its totality including various components both natural and human.
Natural Environment: Land-interior of the earth, rocks and minerals, earth movements and major land forms. (One case study related with earthquakes to be introduced)	To explain the components of natural environment. To appreciate the interdependence of these components and their importance in our life To appreciate the develop sensitivity towards environment.

Air- composition, structure of the atmosphere, elements of weather and climate- temperature, pressure, moisture and winds. (one case study related with cyclones to be introduced)	To understand about atmosphere and its elements.
Water- fresh and saline, distribution of major water bodies, ocean waters and their circulation. (one case study related with tsunamis to be introduced)	To know about distribution of water on the earth.
Natural Vegetation and Wild Life	To find out the nature of diverse flora and fauna
Human Environment: settlement, transport and communication.	To appreciate the need of transport and communication for developments making today's world.
Human-Environment Interaction; Case studies- life in deserts- Sahara and Ladakh; life in tropical and subtropical regions- Amazon and Ganga-Brahmaputra; Life in temperate regions- Prairies and Veldts.	To explain the relationship between natural environment and human habitation.

Q13. Prepare a lesson plan for teaching-learning on topic of 'transport' related to geographical areas in India.

Ans. Usually, every teacher will go to class after making enough preparation. Planning a lesson is as important as teaching a lesson. The teacher should look into the chapter on transport and identify the focal points. A few of them are given below:

- Transport plays a very important role in our daily life.
- Availability of transport depends on various factors.
- There are different ways and means of transport.
- Roadways are common means of transport in north-eastern states.
- Roadways are of different ways – International highways, national highways, state highways, district roads and village roads.

Having identified and sequenced the content points, it is necessary to state the learning objectives based on the content, which are as follows:

- To explore the importance of transport
- To identify the different modes of transport
- To identify the types of roads

Before discussing any topic in the class, it is advisable to use the experiences of the students related to that topic. Now we see how to generate discussion using their experience.

Students would have experienced 'road blockage' due to land slide/ human action or any other. Let them talk about reasons for and the effect of road blockage.

Fig. 2.3: Road Blockage

Discussion may begin with some questions. Few examples are given below:

- Who have experienced road blockage?
- Where was the road blockage?
- How long was it?
- Why did the road blockage happen?
- How did it affect your movement?
- How does it affect the regular work of the people?

After answering the above questions, students are required to make intelligent guessing. Therefore, ask them 'suppose the road blockage continues for a week, what will happen to the daily life of the people? In what ways can we over come road blockage?

The above activity will enable the students to understand the importance of transport. Now, the teacher should ask the students to name some materials of daily use. Let it be listed on the Black board. Get it classified into locally grown/made and non-local. Ask them from where they get those things. How do they procure them, how do those things reach the shops and so on? These questions to be asked with the intention of getting the term 'transport' explained the students.

Display the maps of transport- Roadways, Railways, Waterways and Airways of India. Allow them to find the mode of transport available in North-east India, Jammu and Kashmir, Himachal Pradesh, Uttarakhand, etc. List them on the black board. The teacher may help the students in drawing the diagram i.e. Fig. after sufficient discussion on modes of transport.

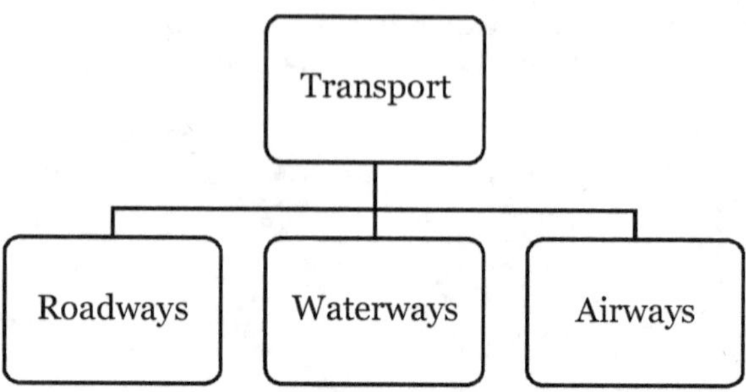

Fig. 2.4: Modes of Transport

They may also be asked to name important places connected through different modes of transport.

Once the learners are introduced to the modes of transport, they may be allowed to plan for exploration and discussion on 'transport in India'. Students can be asked to group themselves in to desired number of groups to work on four modes of transport with approximately equal number of students in each of the groups. Give them enough time and freedom to choose one way of transport. They are to be asked to collect information, pictures and maps showing the availability of mode of transport chosen by them. The teacher will guide them at appropriate intervals. At the end of investigation, each group will arrange the materials and information collected by them and presents it to the class followed by a discussion.

The teacher may now move to advantages of transport by conducting a brainstorming session. Ask every student to tell at least one advantage of transport. List them on the black board. S/he can underline three to four advantages on the black board, which lead to economic development (like transport of minerals, consumer goods) and ask the students how transport contributes to the development of the Country. Let the students know that all places are not self-sufficient in terms of production of different goods. They are always inter-dependent. Inter-dependence can be at any level – local, regional, national, and international. Let the students find out what things are sent out from their place and what things are brought into their place from other places.

Q14. Discuss 'social and political life' as a component of social science at elementary stage.

Ans. At the primary stage (class I-V), social sciences are taught to the children as an integrated component of 'environmental studies' curriculum. Environmental studies curriculum, at this stage, is a composite instructional area, which includes contents from social sciences, general sciences and/or many other subjects. At the upper primary level, social science curriculum has been prepared in an integrated fashion emphasizing on relationship across the component subjects and different grades. In other words, it means, social science curriculum at the upper primary stage has been integrated across the subject areas (i.e. history, geography, and social and political life) and across the grades (from class VI to VIII).

Learning **history** *at upper primary stage:* Learning history acquaints learners with the developments in different parts of India and in different parts of the world in relation to the time.

Learning of **geography** *at upper primary stage:* Learning of geography acquaints learners with the issues of nature, environment, resources, materials etc. in relation to space (starting from local to global level).

Learning of **social and political** *life at upper primary stage:* At upper primary stage, social and political life acts as an integrated subject of political science/economics/sociology.

Q15. Justify 'social and political life' as an integrated subject of political science/economics/sociology.

Ans. At upper primary stage, Social and Political life (SPL) is a new learning area of social science curriculum replacing the earlier learning area of 'Civics'. NCF (2005) remarked that, "Civics appeared in the Indian school curriculum in the colonial period against the background of increasing 'disloyalty' among Indians towards the Raj. Emphasis on obedience and loyalty were the key features of civics".

SPL uses practical situations to teach concepts because it recognizes that children learn best through concrete experiences. It uses materials that draw upon the experimental understanding of familial and social issues that middle school children bring to the classroom.

Social and Political Life (SPL) draws its contents mainly from three disciplines i.e. political science, economics and sociology. **Political Science** is concerned with the contents relating to democracy, authority, governance, etc. of the individuals in society/state. At this stage, teaching of political science acquaints students mainly with democratic values, mostly focusing on values enshrined in the Indian constitution. **Economics** is the subject which is related to issues like production, consumption, distribution, marketing, exchange of goods and services, etc. **Sociology** makes the child to be an important member of civic society, removing the barriers of caste, class, religion, etc.

Q16. Delineate approaches adopted by social scientists in understanding political science.

Or

Differentiate between traditional approaches and modern approaches to Political Science.

Or

Mention any *one* modern approach of teaching of Political Science.									**[April-2016, Q.No.-24]**

Ans. To understand political science, prominent classification of approaches is traditional and modern approaches have become quite dominant.

The traditional approaches to Political Science were widely prevalent till the outbreak of the Second World War. These approaches were mainly related to the traditional view of politics which emphasised the study of the state and government. Therefore, traditional approaches are primarily concerned with the study of the organisation and activities of the state and principles and the ideas which underlie political organisations and activities. These approaches were normative and idealistic. To minimise the deficiencies of the traditional approaches, various new approaches have been advocated by the new political thinkers. These new approaches are regarded as the "modern approaches" to the study of Political Science. Many thinkers regard these approaches as a reaction against the traditional approaches. These approaches are mainly concerned with scientific study of politics.

Table 2.5: Difference between Traditional Approach and Modern Approach

Traditional approaches	Modern approaches
Define political science as the study of state and its governmental institutions	Define political science as the study of power and decision making of political behavior
Concentrates on formal apparatus of politics : government, institutions, constitutions etc.	See politics as an activity or a process service.
Defines political science as a subjective, theoretical and purpose oriented task	Define political science as an objective, scientific and process oriented task
More philosophical in nature	More analytic in nature
See political science as non observable and value loaded subject	See political science as observable and value free subject
Prescriptive and normative. Aim at the achievement of good society	Insist on quantitative and inductive approach. Aim at making politics a scientific body of knowledge
Basically taxonomic and focus on institutions as the main instrument of social change and control	Focus on extra political factors and conditions which affect the behaviour of political events and institutes.

In many situations, there is an interaction between both these two categories of approaches. There are many traditional and modern approaches to understand political science. Following are two important traditional approaches (philosophical and legal-institutional approach) two important modern approaches (behavioural and psychological approach) to understand political science:

Philosophical Approach: This approach is regarded as the oldest approach to the study of Political Science. The emergence of this approach can be traced back to the times of the Greek philosophers like Plato and Aristotle. Leo Strauss was one of the main advocates of the philosophical approach. He believes that "the philosophy is the quest for wisdom and political philosophy is the attempt truly to know about the nature of political things and the right or good political order." This approach firmly believes that the values cannot be separated from the study of politics. Therefore, its main concern is to judge what is good or bad in any political society. It is mainly an ethical and normative study of politics and, thus, idealistic. It deals with the problems of the nature and functions of the state, citizenship, rights and duties, etc. The advocates of this approach firmly believe that political philosophy is closely linked with the political ideologies. Therefore, they are of the opinion that a political scientist must have the knowledge of good life and good society. Political philosophy helps in setting up of a good political order.

Legal-institutional (constitutional) Approach: Legal approach regards the state as the fundamental organisation for the creation and enforcement of laws. Therefore, this approach is concerned with the legal process, legal bodies or institutions, justice and independence of judiciary. The advocates of this approach are Cicero, Jean Bodin, Thomas Hobbes, Jeremy Bentham, John Austin, Dicey and Sir Henry Maine. Institutional approach is a very old and important approach to the study of Political Science. This approach mainly deals with the formal aspects of government and politics emphasises the study of the political institutions and structures. Thus, the institutional approach is concerned with the study of the formal structures like legislature, executive, judiciary, political parties, interest groups, etc. The advocates of this approach include both ancient and modern political thinkers. Among the ancient thinkers Aristotle is an important contributor to this approach while the modern thinkers include James Bryce, Bentley, Walter Bagehot, Harold Laski, etc.

Behavioural Approach: Among the modern empirical approach, the behavioural approach, to study political science, grabbed notable place. Most eminent exponents of this approach are David Eatson, Robert A. Dahl, E. M. Kirkpatrick, and Heinz Eulau. Behavioural approach is political theory which is the result of increasing attention given to behaviour of ordinary man. Theorist, Kirkpatrick stated that traditional approaches accepted institution as the basic unit of research but behavioural approach considers the behaviour of individual in political situation as the basis (K. Sarmah, 2007).

Psychological Approach: There is a strong link between politics and psychology. Psychologists usually study the political behaviour of individuals and factors leading to such behaviour. Psychological approach became dominant in the field of political science after publication of Graham Wallas' Human Nature in Politics (1908)' which laid emphasis on socio-psychological foundation of political science. Psychologists also study why certain individuals behave in a certain way. In simple form, psychology studies the behaviour, attitude of the voter and after studying various aspects, the researchers draw conclusions which very often serve the purpose of political leaders. It is not an overstatement to hold that the foundation of behaviouralism is psychology of the individuals. Presently, political scientists are eager to know how motives and emotions work in the field of political activity. Sometimes, the psychologists focus upon the group behaviour.

Besides these approaches, there are many other approaches to understand the Political Science like, comparative approach, system analysis approach, structural-functional analysis approach, Marxian approach, etc.

Q17. Define Economics. Describe the methods/approaches adopted by social scientists in understanding economics.

Ans. Economics is quite an old discipline. Its development in the contemporary form was a continuous process. Perhaps the beginning was made by the Greek philosopher, Aristotle, who, in his two books, *Economica* confined the study of economics to household management and acquiring, guarding and making proper use of wealth. In fact, the word 'economics' has been derived from the Greek words oikos meaning a house and 'nemein' meaning to manage. So, economics means managing a household with limited funds. The concept of frugal use of one's limited resources in managing a household has been extended to macro level which gave birth to the term 'economy' implying the manner in which a particular society organises its resources for maximum production of desired goods.

There is no consensus among economists about a precise definition of economics. Several approaches have been followed in the past in this regard. The current position is that there are perhaps, as many specific definitions as there are economics instructors.

Though there are various approaches used by economists in understanding economies, but among them few approaches are quite significant and there are as follows:

(1) **Wealth approach of Adam Smith:** Economics, as a study of wealth, received great support from the Father of economics, Adam Smith, in the late eighteenth century. Adam smith (1723-1790), in his book "An Inquiry into Nature and Causes of Wealth of Nations" (1776) defined economics as the science of wealth. He explained how a nation's wealth is created. He considered that the individual in the society wants to promote only his own gain and in this, he is led by an "invisible hand" to promote the interests of the society though he has no real intention to promote the society's interests.

Production and expansion of wealth as the subject matter of economics has been stated by Adam Smith; but, the critics of this definition claimed that acquisition of wealth being the motive of human being's, is totally baseless. In a civilized society, human activities are guided by many other motives except acquisition of wealth. Further, critics opined that wealth definition of Adam Smith gave much stress on wealth but not on human welfare. In other words, wealth approach failed to prove human welfare as the main objective of economics.

(2) **Welfare approach of Alfred Marshall:** Alfred Marshall (1842-1924) wrote a book "Principles of Economics" (1890) in which he defined "Political Economy" or Economics is a study of mankind in the ordinary business of life; it examines that part

of individual and social action which is most closely connected with the attainment and with the use of the material requisites of well being". Marshall's definitions are as follows:

(i) According to Marshall, economics is a study of mankind in the ordinary business of life, i.e., economic aspect of human life.

(ii) Economics studies both individual and social actions aimed at promoting economic welfare of people.

(iii) Marshall makes a distinction between two types of things, viz. material things and immaterial things. Material things are those that can be seen, felt and touched. Immaterial things are those that cannot be seen, felt and touched.

Criticism:

(a) Marshall considered only material things. But immaterial things, such as the services of a doctor, a teacher and so on, also promote welfare of the people.

(b) Marshall makes a distinction between those things that are capable of promoting welfare of people and those things that are not capable of promoting welfare of people. But anything, (E.g.) liquor, that is not capable of promoting welfare but commands a price, comes under the purview of economics.

(c) Marshall's definition is based on the concept of welfare. But there is no clear-cut definition of welfare.

(3) Scarcity and choice approach of Lionel Robbins: Lionel Robbins published a book "An Essay on the Nature and Significance of Economic Science" in 1932. According to him, "economics is a science which studies human behaviour as a relationship between ends and scarce means which have alternative uses". The major features of Robbins' definition are as follows:

(i) Ends refer to human wants. Human beings have unlimited number of wants.

(ii) Resources or means, on the other hand, are limited or scarce in supply. There is scarcity of a commodity, if its demand is greater than its supply. In other words, the scarcity of a commodity is to be considered only in relation to its demand.

(iii) The scarce means are capable of having alternative uses. Hence, anyone will choose the resource that will satisfy his particular want. Thus, economics, according to Robbins, is a science of choice.

Criticism:

(a) Robbins does not make any distinction between goods conducive to human welfare and goods that are not conducive to human welfare. In the production of rice and alcoholic drink, scarce resources are used. But the production of rice promotes human welfare while production of alcoholic drinks is not conducive to human welfare. However, Robbins concludes that economics is neutral between ends.

(b)   In economics, we not only study the micro economic aspects like how resources are allocated and how price is determined, but we also study the macro-economic aspect like how national income is generated. But, Robbins has reduced economics merely to theory of resource allocation.

(c)   Robbins definition does not cover the theory of economic growth and development.

(4) Growth approach of Samuelson: Prof. Paul Samuelson defined economics as "the study of how men and society choose, with or without the use of money, to employ scarce productive resources which could have alternative uses, to produce various commodities over time, and distribute them for consumption, now and in the future among various people and groups of society".

The major implications of this definition are as follows:

(i)   Samuelson has made his definition dynamic by including the element of time in it. Therefore, it covers the theory of economic growth.

(ii)   Samuelson stressed the problem of scarcity of means in relation to unlimited ends. Not only the means are scarce, but they could also be put to alternative uses.

(iii)   The definition covers various aspects like production, distribution and consumption.

Q18. Elucidate methods/approaches adopted by social scientists in understanding sociology.

Ans. Sociology studies human societies, their interactions, and the processes that preserve and change them. It does this by examining the dynamics of constituent parts of societies such as institutions, communities, populations, and gender, racial, or age groups. Sociology also studies social status or stratification, social movements, and social change, as well as societal disorder in the form of crime, deviance, and revolution.

There isn't a single method/approach, which is used by the social scientists to study the society; rather, social scientists use numerous methods to study the society. Each method has its own strengths and limitations depending upon the context of studying the society. Following are the important methods/approaches used by the social scientists in understanding sociology:

(1) Functionalist approach: Functionalist approach has profound influence on modern sociological theorising. This method, in fact, is an outcome of the reaction against evolutionary method. Functionalist approach to study society refers to 'the study of the society/social phenomenon from the point of the functions of the society/social phenomenon (or the elements of the society/social phenomenon)'. Functions of a system refer to the activities which are performed by the system (or its elements) in order to achieve healthy maintenance of the system. This approach is based upon the assumption that a system is based upon a number of its constituent parts. Each part of the system is interrelated with other parts of the system. The function of a part of the system is understood in relation to functions of the other parts of the system. In the same way, if society is a system, its constituent parts are religion, economy, politics, etc. Auguste Comte and Herbert Spence laid the foundation for studying the society from functionalist perspective. Durkheim was the champion in using this method in studying the social phenomenon. The sociologist like Radcliffe Brown and Malinowski highly admired this approach in studying the social phenomenon.

(2) **Statistical approach:** Statistical approach is used to study the social phenomenon in quantitative and objective ways. Through this approach, the social issues relating to birth and death, divorce, crime, migration, economic condition, public opinion, etc. can nicely be studied. This approach is in much use in order to disclose relationship among different aspects of social phenomenon. It is true that most social data are qualitative, but, still the social scientists are trying their best to make such data quantitative and objective by the meaningful use of the statistical method. Sociologists like Giddings and many others have emphasised the use of this approach in conducting sociological researches.

(3) **Historical approach:** Historical method was by founders of sociology like Auguste Comte, Herbert Spencer and Karl Marx. In recent times, the sociologist like Hothouse, Westermarck and F. Oppenheimer strongly support this method. Historical sociology (sociology based on historical method) studies societies of remote as well as recent past to discover origins of, and find explanations for, our present way of life. Historical approach to study of the society basically follows two forms i.e. (i) historical approach is influenced by biological theory of evolution, and (ii) historical approach influence by economic interpretations. The first approach concentrates on the issues relating to the origin and development of societies. Comte and Spencer used this approach to study the society. The second approach is basically used by Max Weber in his studies of origin of capitalism, the development of modern bureaucracy and the economic influence of the world religions.

    (4) Comparative approach: In order to eliminate the factors which are not essential and arrive at the factors which are essential, comparative approach uses/applies logical principles on social phenomenon. Comparative approach in the field of sociology studies past or existing societies and social institutions by a process of selection, comparison and elimination in order to arrive at proper generalisation. In natural science, scientist can establish causal connection by experiment. But in study of social setting, experiment is hardly possible. Hence, social scientists establish causal connections by examining cases in which two or more phenomena are simultaneously present or absent. Thus, comparative method in the field of social science shows how certain social phenomena are frequently associated with each other or frequently occur in a regular order of succession. To study the social phenomenon, this approach was frequently used by Durkheim, Max Weber and other sociologists.

Q19. Justify the significance of social and political life as a part of social science curriculum. Also, enlist the objectives of the learning of social and political life.

Or

Name any *two* objectives of social and political life at school level.   **[April-2016, Q.No.-37]**

Or

Explain any five objectives of learning about social and political life as part of Social Science curriculum at upper primary level.   **[October-2016, Q.No.-41]**

Ans. Like 'history' and 'geography', a significant aspect of social science is constituted by 'social and political life'. While history has been included in social science curriculum in order to make the children aware their rich past at different points of time, geography has been included in social science curriculum in order to make the children aware of physical, environmental and socio-cultural features of their surroundings, social and political life has been included in social science curriculum in order to make the children aware of various aspects of their social, political and economic life. At the upper primary level, the learning of social and political life is generally concerned with these objectives:

- To make the learners active participants of society.
- To help the learners solve different controversial socio-political and economic issues.
- To promote the values of peace and understanding among the learners.
- To promote social, political and economic values among the learners.
- To develop the values of patriotism, co-operation and tolerance among the learners.

- To inculcate the democratic and constitutional values in the learners.
- To make the learners familiar with the social, political and economic institutions.

National Focus Group on Teaching of Social Sciences (2006) state the rationale of 'social and political life' as below:

At the elementary stage, the idea is to introduce students to various aspects of political, social and economic life. This will be done through a preliminary focus on certain key concepts, knowledge of which is essential to understand the functioning of Indian democracy. These concepts will be explained using imaginary narratives that allow children to draw connections between these and their everyday experiences. There will be no attempt made at this level to cover all aspects of India's democratic structure, but rather the effort is more to provide an overview with which the child learns to critically engage by constructing herself as an interested citizen of a vibrant and ongoing democratic process. The focus on the real-life functioning of institutions and ideals is to enable the child to grasp the deep interconnectedness between the political and social aspects of her everyday life, as well as the impact of these two in the realm of economic decision-making.

Q20. Illustrate the pedagogical principles of learning social and political life in social science curriculum.

Ans. Basically, an interactive and experimental pedagogic situation is required in learning of social and political life. The learning must be related with the real life situations of the learners. The cultural and social contexts of the learner must be given high priority in whole teaching learning process of social and political life. The pedagogy used for learning of this area must facilitate the creativity, critical understanding, and problem solving ability of the learners. The pedagogy of this area must follow the learning by playing, learning by enjoying and learning by doing. By keeping the learner at the central place of teaching learning, the pedagogy must be learner oriented.

We can see below how the learning of social and political life follows an activity oriented teaching learning pedagogy.

Activity Based Learning on Good Social Habits: This is a classroom-based activity. The purpose of this activity is to develop good social habits among learners and eliminate bad social habits among them. The details of the activity are given under the following headings/points.

(1) Activity Profile:

Class	:	VI level
Learning Area	:	'Social and Political Life' area of Social Science Curriculum
Content of Learning	:	Good social habits
Main learning objective	:	Developing good social habits among learners and eliminating bad social habits among them.
Materials required	:	Some pictures relating to good

Strategy	:	social habits and bad social habits Putting right (✓) or cross (x) against appropriate pictures
Mode	:	Individualised

Fig. 2.5

(2) Activity Followed: In this activity, the teacher will guide the learners in this way:

Dear learners. A number of pictures are given in the above box. All such pictures characterize some social habits performed by the individuals in the society. Choose the appropriate pictures which show the good social habits and put tick mark (✓) in right side of those pictures, and put cross mark (x) in the right side of those pictures which are related to bad social habits.

(3) Activity based Learning Assignments: These learning assignments are for the learners. For performing these learning assignments, the teacher will guide the learners in the following way:

Below is given a number of tasks for you (learners), which are very interesting. Do complete the tasks and submit them for discussion and analysis.

(i)   Prepare a small story and title the story as ' Good social habits'

(ii)   Write an essay on 'Evil effects of bad social habits'.

(iii)   Prepare some posters on good social habits.

(iv)   Enlist the bad social habits practiced in your school premise and report them to your class teacher.

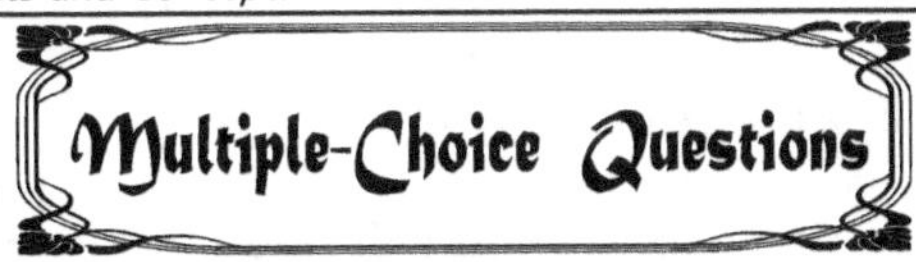

Q1. Who is known as 'Father of History'?
 (a) Alexander   (b) Aristotle
 (c) Herodotus   (d) Henary Johnson
Ans. (c) Herodotus

Q2. Aristotle was a native of ______.
 (a) Greece   (b) France
 (c) England   (d) Spain
Ans. (a) Greece

Q3. The Vedas, the Epics and the Puranas are involved in which sources?
 (a) Archaeological sources   (b) Literary sources
 (c) Secular literature   (d) Foreign testimony
Ans. (b) Literary sources

Q4. Who wrote *Arthashastra*?
 (a) Kautilya   (b) Chandragupta Maurya
 (c) Euripides   (d) Leonardo da Vinci
Ans. (a) Kautilya

Q5. "Geography is concerned with the description and explanation of the areal differentiation of the earth surface". Who said this line?
 (a) Hettner   (b) Richard Hartshorne
 (c) Peter Monaghan   (d) None of the above
Ans. (b) Richard Hartshorne

Q6. Among the following, which one is included in Biogeography?
 (a) Zoo Geography
 (b) Environmental Geography
 (c) Plant Geography
 (d) All of the above
Ans. (d) All of the above

Q7. Which among the following is not included in the methods and techniques of Regional Geography?
 (a) Field Survey Methods
 (b) Methods to study the society
 (c) Cartography Including Computer Cartography
 (d) Quantitative Techniques/statistical Methods
Ans. (b) Methods to study the society

Q8. What is the full form of 'GPS'?
 (a) Geographic Positioning System
 (b) Global Positioning Stand

(c) Global Positioning System

(d) General Positioning System

Ans. (c) Global Positioning System

Q9. **At the primary level, social science is included in our school curriculum in the form of _____.**

(a) Environmental Studies

(b) Environmental Response Team

(c) Environmental Management System

(d) None of the above

Ans. (a) Environmental Studies

Q10. **Who wrote the book 'Leviathan'?**

(a) Plato　　　　　　　**(b) Hobbes**

(c) Locke　　　　　　　**(d) Aristotle**

Ans. (b) Hobbes

Q11. **Graham Wallas 'Human Nature in Politics' was published in which year?**

(a) 1906　　　　　　　**(b) 1901**

(c) 1904　　　　　　　**(d) 1908**

Ans. (d) 1908

Q12. **Who is considered as the father of Economics?**

(a) Adam Smith　　　　　**(b) Lionel Robbins**

(c) Karl Marx　　　　　　**(d) Alfred Marshall**

Ans. (a) Adam Smith

Q13. **Political science makes the child familiar with ________.**

(a) Economic processes and participation

(b) Democratic processes and participation

(c) Political processes and participation

(d) Geographic processes and participation

Ans. (b) Democratic processes and participation

Q14. **___________uses/applies logical principles on social phenomenon in order to eliminate the factors which are not essential and arrive at the factors which are essential.**

(a) Comparative approach　　　**(b) Political approach**

(c) Systematic approach　　　　**(d) All of above**

Ans. (a) Comparative approach

☺☺☺

Issues in Pedagogy of Social Sciences

INTRODUCTION

The contents of social sciences drawn from the disciplines of history, geography, political science, and economics, e.g. community, demography, culture, development, environment and utility are formed through child's engagement in activities, experience and illustration. Social science teaching based on these, creates cognitive capacities of the learners such as observation, identification and classification that are fundamental to understanding of social issues, e.g. poverty, illiteracy, population growth, communalism. Therefore, organisation of curriculum and method of teaching social sciences at different levels of education should take into account the development stage as well as environment of the child. The teaching based on this can create cognitive capacity within the child that helps him in understanding the socio-economic problems of society. In our country children belonging to three major socio-cultural backgrounds, namely urban, rural and tribal are exposed to different social issues, concepts and have the unique way of concept formation. The approaches to teaching, including pedagogy and resources, therefore, should vary accordingly.

Q1. **Briefly describe about diversity in India. Elucidate the dimensions of socio-cultural diversity including religious and linguistic diversity among learners.**

Or

How many languages are used in India?

[April-2016, Q.No.-1]

Ans. India is one of the vast countries with extraordinary characteristics and diversity in terms of its geographical, linguistic, religious, social-cultural features, etc. In the words of Raj Thackrey, *"India is like Europe. This means there is one currency and numerous languages and cultures. This is "Europe" made up of various cultures."*

We see various types of diversity in India, for example those in eating habits, dresses and costumes, religion, customs, etc. Such types of diversity are also commonly seen in many parts of the world. Unity implies oneness or a sense of we-ness, it holds tightly together the various relationships of ethnic groups or institutions in a dovetailed manner through the bonds of contrived structures, norms and values. The sources of diversity in India may be traced through a variety of ways, the most obvious being the ethnic origins, religions, castes, tribes, languages, social customs, cultural and sub cultural beliefs, political philosophies and ideologies, geographical variations, etc.

In India, there has been among continual interaction communities and they have constantly maintained cultural linkages, particularly by sharing resources, traits, and space (observable at grassroot level). These trends, indeed, shaped the unique pattern of India's composite heritage and cultural unity. Research reveals that popular cultural traits such as, food habits, marriage patterns, social customs, social organization, economy and occupation cut across regions. Hindus share 96.77% traits with Muslims, 91.19% with Buddhists, 89.99% with Sikhs and 77.46% with Janis. Muslims share 91.18 % traits with Buddhists, 89.95% with Sikhs. Janis shares 81.34 % traits with Buddhists. The Scheduled Tribes (ST) share 96.61 % traits with Other Backward Castes (OBCs), 95.82% with Muslims, 91.69% with Buddhists, 91.29 % with Scheduled Castes (SCs), 88.20 % with Sikhs (K.S. Singh, 1996).

Following are the dimensions of socio-cultural diversity:

(1) **Religious Diversity:** Religion is one of the key facets of diversity, along with race, gender, disability and age. India is a secular, multi-religious and multicultural country. It's a land from where important religions namely Hinduism, Buddhism, Sikhism and Jainism have originated at the same time and have flourished and survived the influence of religions like Islam and Christianity and is home to several indigenous faiths tribal religions. According to the 2011 census, 79.8% of the population of India practices Hinduism and 14.2% adheres to Islam, while the remaining 6% adheres to other religions (Christianity, Sikhism, Buddhism, Jainism and various indigenous ethnically-bound faiths). Christianity is the 3rd largest religion in India.

Table 3.1: India's Population according to Census, 2011

Religion	Percent	Estimated
All Religion	100.00 %	121 Crores
Hindu	79.80 %	96.62 Crores
Muslim	14.23 %	17.22 Crores
Christian	2.30 %	2.78 Crores
Sikh	1.72 %	2.08 Crores
Buddhist	0.70 %	84.43 Lakhs
Jain	0.37 %	44.52 Lakhs
Other Religion	0.66 %	79.38 Lakhs
Not Stated	0.24 %	28.67 Lakhs

(2) Linguistic Diversity: India is a multilingual country and the constitution accords to protect the multilingual nature of India. In terms of linguistic diversity, it has a variety of languages and dialects. Most languages in India belong to one of the four language families: Indo-Aryan (spoken by 75% of population, of which Hindi is the most widely spoken language in India), Dravidian (spoken by 20%), Tibeto-Burmese and Austro-Asiatic. According to the 2001 Indian Census, there are a total of 122 major languages and 234 identifiable mother tongues. Of these, 29 languages have more than a million native speakers, 60 have more than 100,000 and 122 have more than 10,000 native speakers. However, many languages which are spoken by less than 10,000 speakers are not reported in Census. Many among the unreported languages are spoken by tribal communities. Out of the 122 major languages 22 languages are listed under 8th Schedule (this was included in the Constitution in order to provide official status to many Indian languages). Language is one of the principal powerful symbols of identity in India. States in the Indian Union are demarcated on the basis of the principal language spoken. People are identified with certain linguistic, ethnic, religious or cultural groups through ones mother tongue. Moreover, language has been basis for many of the ethnic movements in the country.

Q2. Describe active, constructive involvement of the learners to understand social science issues.

Ans. Active learning is based on a theory of learning called constructivism, which emphasises the fact that learners construct or build their own understanding. Learning is a process of making meaning. Learners replace or adapt their existing knowledge and understanding (based on their prior knowledge) with deeper and more skilled levels of understanding. Skilled teaching is therefore active, providing learning environments, opportunities, interactions, tasks and instruction that foster deep learning.

At the primary state, to develop the understanding of natural and social environment, children should be engaged in activities that would help them. Understanding at this level should be based on observation and illustration rather than abstractions. Illustrations need to be drawn from the children's physical, biological, social and cultural aspects of life. The skills, namely observation, identification and classification are important to become an active learner at this stage.

Subject areas of social science are drawn from history, geography, political science and economics at the upper primary stage. An emphasis is given, at this stage, on issues like poverty, illiteracy, child labour, casteism, environmental pollution that help students explore and understand these issues.

In the Classroom: It is a challenge for teachers to create interesting and challenging learning environments that encourage the active involvement of students. The following are some suggestions as to how this can be done:

- Avoid situations where the students are passive listeners for long periods of time.
- Provide students with hands-on activities, such as experiments, observations, projects, etc.
- Encourage participation in classroom discussions and other collaborative activities.
- Organise school visits to museums and technological parks.
- Allow students to take some control over their own learning. Taking control over one's learning means allowing students to make some decisions about what to learn and how.
- Assist students in creating learning goals that are consistent with their interests and future aspirations.

Q3. Explain the social participation of the learners in social activities of school.

Ans. For many researchers, social participation is the main activity through which learning occurs. Social activity and participation begin early on. Parents interact with their children and through these interactions children acquire the behabaviours that enable them to become effective members of society. According to the psychologist Lev Vygotsky, the way children learn is by internalising the activities, habits, vocabulary and ideas of the members of the community in which they grow up.

The establishment of a fruitful collaborative and co-operative atmosphere is an essential part of school learning. Research has shown that social collaboration can boost student achievement, provided that the kinds of interactions that are encouraged contribute to learning. Finally, social activities are interesting in their own right and help to keep students involved in their own right and help to keep students involved in their academic work. Students work harder to improve the quality of their products (essays, projects, artwork, etc.) when they know that they will be shared with other students.

In the Classroom: Teachers can do many things to encourage social participation in ways that facilitate learning:

- They can assign students to work in groups and assume the role of a coach/co-ordinator who provides guidance and support to the groups.

- They can create a classroom environment that includes group workspaces where resources are shared.
- Through modeling and coaching, they can teach students how to co-operate with each other.
- They can create circumstances for students to interact with each other, to express their opinions and to evaluate other students' arguments.
- An important aspect of social learning is to link the school to the community at large. In this way, students' opportunities for social participation are enlarged.

Q4. Delineate about the participation of children in meaningful activities at school.

Ans. Many school activities are not meaningful since students understand neither why they are doing them nor what their purpose and usefulness is. Sometimes school activities are not meaningful because they are not culturally appropriate. Many schools are communities where children from diverse cultures learn together. There are systematic cultural differences in practices, in habits, in social roles, etc., that influence learning. Sometimes meaningful activities for students coming from one cultural group are not meaningful to students who are coming from another cultural group.

In the Classroom: Teachers can make classroom activities more meaningful by situating them in an authentic context. An example of an authentic context is one in which the activity is typically used in real life. For example, students can improve their oral language and communication skills by participating in debates. They can improve their writing skills by being involved in the preparation of a classroom newspaper. Students can learn science by participating in a community or school environmental project. The school can be in contact with local scientists and invite them to lecture, or allow the students to visit their laboratories.

It is also important for teachers to be aware of the cultural differences of the children in their classroom and to respect these differences. They must see them as strengths to build on, rather than as defects. Children will feel differently in the classroom if their culture is reflected in the common activities. School routines that are unfamiliar to some children can be introduced gradually so that the transition can be less traumatic for ethnically diverse groups.

Q5. Describe learners' ability to relate new information to prior knowledge. Also, explain as a teacher how do you help them to relate their prior knowledge to the task at hand?

Or

Why is it necessary to relate new information with prior knowledge? Give one reason.   [October-2016, Q.No.-26]

Ans. The idea that people's ability to learn something new follows from what they already know is not new, but more recent research findings have shown that the ability to relate new information to prior knowledge is critical for learning. It is not possible for someone to understand, remember or learn something that is completely unfamiliar. Some prior knowledge is necessary to understand the task at hand. But having the prerequisite prior knowledge is still not sufficient to ensure adequate results. People must activate their prior knowledge in order to be able to use it for understanding and for learning. Research shows that students do not consistently see the relationships between new material that they read and what they already know. Research also shows that learning is enhanced when teachers pay close attention to the prior knowledge of the learner and use this knowledge as the starting point for instruction.

In the Classroom: Teachers can help students to activate prior knowledge and use it for the task at hand. This can be done in a number of ways:

- Teachers can discuss the content of a lesson before starting in order to ensure that the students have the necessary prior knowledge and in order to activate this knowledge.
- Often students' prior knowledge is incomplete or there are false beliefs and critical misconceptions. Teachers do not simply need to know that students know something about the topic to be introduced. They need to investigate students' prior knowledge in detail so that false beliefs and misconceptions can be identified.
- Teachers may need to go back to cover important prerequisite material or ask the students to do some preparatory work on their own.
- Teachers can ask the kind of question that helps students see relationships between what they are reading and what they already know.
- Effective teachers can help students to grasp relationships and make connections. They can do so by providing a model or a scaffold that students can use as support in their efforts to improve their performance.

Q6. Identify Piaget's theory of cognitive development.

Ans. Based on his studies, Piaget put forth clearly demarcated sequential stages in cognitive development in children, namely:

- Sensory motor period (Birth to 2 years)
- Pre-operational period (2-7 years)
- Concrete operational period (7-11 years)
- Formal operational period (11-15 years)

(1) **Sensory Motor Stage (Birth to 2 years):** During this stage, infants and toddlers acquire knowledge through sensory experiences and manipulating objects. It was his observations of his daughter and nephew that heavily influenced his conception of this stage. At this point in development, a child's intelligence consists of their basic motor and sensory explorations of the world. Piaget believed that developing object permanence or object constancy, the understanding that objects continue to exist even when they cannot be seen, was an important element at this point of development. By learning that objects are separate and distinct entities and that they have an existence of

their own outside of individual perception, children are then able to begin to attach names and words to objects.

(2) **Pre-operational stage (Ages 2 to 7):** At this stage, kids learn through pretend play but still struggle with logic and taking the point of view of other people. They also often struggle with understanding the ideal of constancy. For example, a researcher might take a lump of clay, divide it into two equal pieces, and then give a child the choice between two pieces of clay to play with. One piece of clay is rolled into a compact ball while the other is smashed into a flat pancake shape. Since the flat shape looks larger, the preoperational child will likely choose that piece even though the two pieces are exactly the same size.

(3) **Concrete operational stage (7-11 Years):** This stage is differentiated from the pre-operational stage in terms of the development of logical thinking in the children. Piaget believes that a child is able to manipulate and organise information during this period. Concrete operational child uses written words and numbers to symbolise them. This stage is characterised by seven types of conservation (number, length, liquid, mass, weight, area and volume), intelligence is demonstrated through logical and systematic manipulation of symbols related to concrete objects.

(4) **Formal operational stage (11 Years and above):** Formal operational stage is characterised by abstract thinking and the beginning of adolescent thinking. During the formal operational stage, a child is engaged in abstract thinking. S/he does not take anything for granted. Formal operations consist of four overlapping logical abilities, namely (i) Hypothetico-Deductive Thinking; (ii) Inductive Thinking; (iii) Reflective Thinking and (iv) Inter-propositional Logic.

Q7. **Discuss the concept formation among learners.**

Or

Examine the process of concept formation.

[October-2016, Q.No.-36]

Ans. Concept formation provides students with an opportunity to explore ideas by making connections and seeing relationships between items of information. This method can help students develop and refine their ability to recall and discriminate among key ideas, to see commonalities and identify relationships, to formulate concepts and generalisations, to explain how they have organised data, and to present evidence to support their organisation of the data involved.

The process of concept formation has three important phases:

(1) **Perception:** Experiences or learning in any form is the starting point of the process of concept formation. Our perceptions or imaginary experiences, formal or informal learning, provide opportunities for getting mental images of the objects, persons or events.

(2) Abstraction: The mind analyses the perceived images and synthesizes what is common to all, neglecting what is particular. This process of observing similarities and commonness is named as abstraction.

(3) Generalisation: After making such observation in the form of abstraction for a numbers of times, the child is able to generalize or form a general idea about the common properties of some objects or events. On account of this generalization, he will develop a concept about these things or events.

Concept formation provides children with an opportunity to explore ideas by making items of information. The teacher can help his/her children in concept formation. Here are some suggestions for the teachers:

- Give the students a number of materials-written/thoughts (for example, tell them to think of different animals), or real things, (e.g. seeds, leaves). It is preferable to have the students work with real things.

- Put the students in small groups and ask them to classify or group the materials in a way that makes sense.

- Ask the students to give descriptive labels to their groupings

- Ask the students to explain, with evidence/examples, as to how they have organized the materials.

Q8. Describe the approaches to pedagogy.

Ans. Social science teaching needs to be revitalised towards helping the learner acquire knowledge and skills in an interactive environment. The teaching of social sciences must adopt methods that promote creativity, aesthetics, and critical perspectives, and enable children to draw relationships between past and present, to understand changes taking place in society. Problem solving, dramatisation and role play are some hitherto under explored strategies that could be employed. Teaching should utilise greater resources of audio-visual materials, including photographs, charts and maps, and replicas of archaeological and material cultures. In order to make the process of learning participative there is a need to shift from mere imparting of information to debate and discussion. This approach to learning will keep both the learner and teacher alive to social realities.

Concepts should be clarified to the students through the lived experiences of individuals and communities. It has often been observed that cultural, social and class differences generate their own biases, prejudices and attitudes in classroom contexts. The approach to teaching therefore needs to be open-ended. Teachers should discuss different dimensions of social reality in the class, and work towards creating increasing self-awareness amongst themselves and in the learners.

Q9. What are the general features of a learner-centered social sciences class?

Ans. In learner-centered classrooms, students are directly involved and invested in the discovery of their own knowledge. General features which are expected to be in a social sciences class are as follows:

(1) **Using learners' experiences:** Learners' experiences are good resources for teaching. Using learners' experiences gives learners an opportunity to the learner to express as well as participate in classroom processes.

 Example: When we teach on Processes involved in Agriculture, we can ask students, who have seen those processes, to describe them.

(2) **Going beyond the textbook:** A resourceful teacher will always relate the content to the known environment of the learners. This makes understanding of the content easy.

 Example: When we talk about freedom fighters of India, we may ask the learners to find out about the freedom fighters of their state/region.

(3) **Using community resources:** Community is a storehouse of resources both natural and human. There is a need for strong bondage between the school and the community. This can be achieved by involving the community in school activities. This can be done in two ways. One is taking the learners to the community to experience learning and the other is inviting the community to the school.

 Example: When the community organizes cultural programmes school children can participate in the programme. If the school wants to organise a talk on Health related issues, the local health worker can be invited to address the children.

(4) **Creating space for exploration into social issues:** Making children sensitive to the problems and challenges of the society is one of the objectives of teaching social sciences. Unless the teacher relates the lesson to local issues, children may not understand the issues of their society. Therefore, we are required to create opportunities in social sciences class to explore social issues.

 Example: Today, gender discrimination is social issue. A field study can be under taken by the children by visiting the houses in their neighbourhood to find out the practices followed in gender discrimination. We can plan the study along with the children as to what information need to be collected on gender discrimination, from how many houses, from whom, how to compile the data and to write the findings. Children should be asked to share the work among themselves.

(5) **Referring to Human Rights:** Social Science is a subject which has ample scope for referring to Human Rights. Learners

should be made aware of these rights to create a society that respects people.

Example: Basic Health Facilities is a Human Right. While discussing about Directive Principles of State Policy, we can discuss about how the human right is reflected in these policies.

(6) Creating space for developing life skills: By involving the learners in the process of learning social sciences, teachers are expected to see that they are empowered to face the challenges of life. One of the ways of empowering them is through developing life skills in them. Life skills are the abilities for adaptive and positive behaviour that enable an individual to deal effectively with the demands and challenges of everyday life.

Example: Effective communication is one of the life skills. We can create opportunities in social science class by asking learners to speak on selected topics, conduct subject related co-curricular activities, present travel accounts, maintain school bulletin board, etc.

(7) Using Audio Visual Materials': All of us know that what we see and experience remains for a longer time in our memory than what we hear. This holds good to learning too. As there is lot of content to study in social sciences, if teacher uses only chalk and talk method it is difficult for the children to understand especially the abstract concepts. Audio visual materials have the power of giving life to social sciences class. Even NCF-2005 has recommended for utilizing greater resources of audio visual materials.

Example: While teaching about Cotton/Silk/Jute Textile industry, we can use a video clipping which shows the different stages of the industry from the farmland to marketing of finished goods. If this is not possible, at least a chart with pictures and map showing the location of industrial centers may be shown to learners. Wherever possible, sample may also be brought to class to provide the experience of seeing and feeling.

(8) Respect for multiple views: In India, citizens have the freedom to express their views. It becomes the duty of the listeners to respect their views. This value has to be cultivated in the school by creating learning environment. In Social Sciences, when we discuss about some issues, allow the students to express their views. Provide equal opportunity to everyone. This will encourage every learner to respect others views creating a fearless atmosphere which is conducive to learning.

Example: All of us know that construction of a dam results in submergence of hundreds of villages, displacement of people, deforestation, etc.

This may give rise to an issue like — Should we encourage construction of dams? A platform for debate may be created by us allowing learners to express their views without commenting on anybody's views.

(9) **Use of multilinguism:** Generally, multilingualism is the use of more than one language. In a school system, in a country like ours, where we have thousands of dialects, there are chances of mother tongue of the child being different from the language used for instruction. In such schools, to help the learners to understand the concepts without the barrier of language, a teacher can use the mother tongue of the child. It is not literal translation of whatever is taught in the class for the larger group of children, but occasionally, explaining meaning of the terms in the language of the child. This is possible only when the teacher knows the language of the child. Sometimes help may also be taken from other children if the teacher feels confident that the child will give the right word in the language of the other child.

Example: While introducing important terms in History like, monuments, inscription, archaeological sources, etc. we can try to find words in the language of the child and use them in the class. We can also encourage children to prepare their own dictionary for future use. A multilingual chart in social sciences can be displayed in the class for the benefit of all.

Q10.Discuss those factors, which need to be considered by teacher while selecting a strategy in teaching-learning social sciences.

Ans. Following are those factors, which need to be considered while selecting a strategy in teaching learning social sciences:

(1) **Objectives:** There are some objectives in teaching of any unit. We have to select the strategy depending on the type of objective- knowledge, understanding, application, skill etc.

(2) **Content:** Different strategies are demanded by every content. For example, if the content demands visualising the past, then the strategy would be Storytelling. Like this, we have to analyse the content then decide upon the strategy.

(3) **Availability of resources:** In deciding the strategy, resources play an important role. Teacher may think of a good strategy but if the resources are not available, it is not possible to the teacher to follow the intended strategy. Otherwise, strategy has to be decided on the basis of availability of resources.

(4) **Ability of the students:** For taking any decision, students are central point. Depending on the interest, skill and ability of the students, we will have to select the strategy.

(5) **Resourcefulness of the teacher:** In deciding the teaching strategy and pooling the resources, teacher is a very important person, though the students are also consulted in the process of deciding the strategy. If teacher intends to follow a definite strategy, it will happen because it is s/he who is the director of the class.

Q11. Define 'role play'. What steps are involved in it?

Ans. Role-play is when students play the parts of other people in a situation. It has no defined script but the players have a general idea about what they are going to say. Role cards can be prepared before hand in which the situation, the feelings or the thoughts of the characters are given in the form of points. Learners can also enact a telephonic conversation, an interview, where an employee asks for a raise in salary or an angry person at the booking counter.

Role-play could be preceded by a demonstration by the teacher and a few volunteers or by playing a tape. The points on the role-cards are short phrases or sentences and may be used by the players as the lake-off point. The situations that the role-play recreates may be largely from the learners' experience. Using an unfamiliar or strange situation can also be challenging and interesting. This could be preceded by a discussion on the situation or a sample taped dialogue.

Steps in a Role Play:

(1) Fixing a theme or deciding on a theme which is related to the textual content.

(2) Deciding on the type of roles, the number of students required and developing the conversation in a flexible manner.

(3) A small rehearsal may be organised, if the conversations are involved.

(4) Enacting the role play with or without simple costumes.

(5) Feedback by the teacher and the peers

When we consider a textual content, the steps might change. There may be lessons in the form of drama in the language textbook based on social sciences content. For example, when we want our students to practice the dialogues given in the lesson there isn't much scope for change.

Q12. What is meant by project method? Enlist main principles of project method.

Or

Define the principle of purpose of project method.

[October-2016, Q.No.-27]

Ans. Project method is based on the view that experiences lead to learning. Hence, learners need to explore their environment, manipulate objects in their environment, and thus, learn from direct experiences instead of hearing someone else's experiences in some other environment, narrated by teachers. Thus, learning through this method is relevant and meaningful; and based on interests and abilities of learners. Projects may be assigned to individuals or to groups.

The project needs to be based on several principles. Each of them listed below:

(1) **Principle of purposefulness:** A project must have a definite goal. Random activities will not comprise a project.

(2) **Principle of Action:** By Project Method students get opportunity for free thinking and for work. Child is active from his nature and they get practical knowledge being active.

(3) **Principle of utility:** The project should be useful for the students and also for the community. For example, project to make the community environment clean and green.

(4) **Principle of flexibility:** Learners must have the freedom to choose their projects. These projects should not be imposed on them.

(5) **Principle of activity:** There should be definite activities to be carried out by learners. Activities may, however, also include deskwork like reading, writing, planning, etc.

(6) **Principle of Experience:** The students get different experiences, cooperation, character formation, democratic and civic qualities, quality of working in group get from this Project-Method.

Q13. What are the features of a good project? Also, enumerate steps, merits and demerits of a project method.

Ans. Features of a good project: A good project is that which is interesting to the students to work upon and that which is challenging. It should provide rich experience of working together and develop cooperative spirit. A project which is useful and is completed in a reasonably good time is always appreciated.

Steps of a Project Method: The project method consists in the following steps:

- **Providing a situation:** A Project is never to be forced upon pupils. Situations may be provided by conservations or different topics, discussions on pictures, buildings or cities, by telling stories or taking out children on excursions and educational tours and trips.

- **Choosing a Project:** After a situation has been provided, the next step is the choice of a good project. Only such a project should be selected as many satisfy some real need of the pupils and for the good of all of them. The pupil must feel that the project is their own.

- **Planning:** After suitable choice have been made, the next step is prepare a plan for the execution of the project. The entire planning is to be done by the pupils under the guidance of the teacher, after a good deal of discussion. Each child should be encouraged to participate in the discussion and offer his suggestions. The entire plan should be put in black and white by the pupils in their project book is complete.

- **Executing:** When the plan is ready, the teacher should encourage the pupil to put in into practice. He should ask the pupils to assign duties and distribute work among themselves, according to their individual interests and capacities. Each must be given some duty to do for the successful completion of the project. Then, they should be asked to work in co-operation with one another till the project is complete.

- **Judging or Evaluating:** After the completion of project, the student should be asked to review their work. They should note their mistakes, if any, and see whether they had proceeded, according to the plan or not. It is a sort of self-criticism which is a very important from a training and should never be neglected.

- **Recording:** All the pupils should maintain a project-book in which they should put down a complete record of all the activities, connected with the project. This record will be included the choice of project, its planning, discussions held, difficulties felt, duties assigned, references and books consulted, information gathered, experiences gained, guidance sought, etc. Important points for further references and guidance are also to be noted down. Geographical Project Employed is Schools Geographical project may consist of running of a vegetable stall or cloth, cultivation or ploughing of field, running of a school, an agricultural farm, a post office. Village and town markets are other geographical projects. Another type of project consists in the preparation of models of house, school, railway station, etc.

Merits of Project Method: Merits of project method are as follows:

(1) The student gets the scope to imbibe several social qualities like cooperation and teamwork, group affinity and sacrifice through project work.

(2) Since all the activities of a project are related to the real life experiences, each of such activities is meaningful to the student. Therefore, meaningful learning is always associated with the project method.

(3) Completion of the project gives individuals a sense of accomplishment, which in turn, encourages the student for further learning.

(4) The student enjoys full freedom in conducting a project. This develops self-confidence to act and also promotes a sense of responsibilities among the students.

(5) The project method is based on the principles of active learning. The student gets totally involved in the activity which helps in enhancing his/her knowledge, understanding and skills in real life situation and ultimately in developing a holistic personality.

(6) Interest and motivation for the project activities are spontaneously created and no external persuasion or force is needed to attract the students towards learning.

(7) The student gets acquainted with the types of work which s/he is expected to perform in future. Thus, the project method helps the student in his/her preparation for a future life.

Demerits of Project Method: Following are the limitations of the project method:

(1) It is not always possible to employ it in all subject areas of the curriculum.

(2) It is difficult for an average teacher to plan a project and ensure the participation of all students in it.

(3) There is a lack of proper coordination in the experience/knowledge acquired through project method.

Q14. Describe in brief the role of the teacher in project method.

Ans. The project to be successful must be based on a definite procedure. The first and main responsibility of a teacher is to provide those situations in which they feel a spontaneous urge to solve some of their practical problems. The teacher must discover their interest, tastes, aptitudes and needs.

Teacher should motivate the students in such a manner that there is whole hearted cooperation of students in the process. Teacher helps the students in proper planning of the project and discuss with them all the pros and cons of the project. S/he highlights on the important aspects and hazards of the project.

The teacher supplies clues and also provides information to the students about the sources of materials for the project. S/he also helps the students in evaluating the project and to draw inferences.

The relation of the teacher with his students is very closer in project method than in the ordinary class teaching. The teacher is like a friend, an elder brother who works together with the students and helps them to gain rich experiences. S/he acts in the capacity of a director of the student group and gives all types of necessary directions and does not behave as an autocratic teacher.

Q15. Define 'dramatisation'. Which steps are involved in organising dramatisation?

Ans. Dramatisation means reconstruction of some events or situations, past or present into action and life. It provides scope for expression and imagination, sharpens learning, appeals to emotions and removes complexes. History is a subject which deals with events, human ideas and sentiments which have no material shape. It is impossible to translate them into audio-visual symbols through models or puppets. Dramatisation can best represent those concepts and movements. It is one of the most effective devices that teacher of history can use to provide reality and vividness to his/her instruction in history. A student dramatising a character has to 'feel' like the character and to a degree must become the character. Thus, dramatisation makes teaching meaningful, lively and a joyous activity.

Steps in organising dramatization:
- Determining the theatrical element in the lesson
- Searching and finding a play suited to that theme in the lesson
- Modifying the play to suit the lesson
- Deciding on the students who would fit into the different roles in the drama
- Allotting roles to different students and asking them to copy down their part of the conversation
- Giving time to the students to mug up the conversations and understand the theme of the play
- Rehearsals as many as required
- Rehearsals with costumes
- Enactment of the drama
- Feedback on the suitability of the drama – language, theme, acting, dialogue, etc. In costumes of the dramas may not be custom made or from a theatre company. They may be improvised, somewhat ordinary compared to professional dramas.

Q16. Discuss the concept of cooperative learning.

Or

What is cooperative learning? Enumerate its elements and merits.

Or

Define cooperative learning.   **[October-2016, Q.No.-37]**

Ans. As a practising teacher, one might have observed children discussing their class work, home assignment and other school learning experiences. When a teacher gives them class test, they like to tally their answers; to compare their solutions and also to find out discrepancies. Children also like to express and communicate to other children (peers) their liking or disliking of a subject. They like to share their methods of learning, learning difficulties, supplementary reading book, etc. A teacher might have also experienced that if two or more children of the class live in the same locality or are neighbours, they like to study together at home. Children feel motivated and develop interest while working in groups. In a classroom, if teacher provides a child an opportunity to explain his/her correct solution to other children, s/he feels pride in doing so. Children feel responsible when they are asked to help or teach other children who have achieved less. Teacher would see from his/her own experiences that peer interaction and peer co-operation is the basic need of every child just like curiosity and desire to know new things.

Children enjoy working together and helping each other. At the same time, each child wants to do better than the other child. This 'peer group social psychology' of co-operation and competition can be used to facilitate learning and to achieve objectives, which cannot be achieved through individual and competitive methods (Deutch, 1949). Co-operative learning is based on peer co-operation. Co-operative learning methods make use of goal and reward interdependence. Children perceive that they reach their goal only if the other children also reach their goal. They sink and swim together. Based on these assumptions, more satisfaction and better academic performance are expected.

Features: Key features of cooperative learning are as follows:

- Whenever possible teams include a mix of racial, cultural and gender of students.
- Students work in groups to master academic materials.
- Reward systems are group-oriented rather than individually oriented.
- Groups are heterogeneous consisting of high, average and low achievers.

Elements: Basic and essential elements to cooperative learning are:

(1) Positive interdependence:
   (i) Students must fully participate and put forth effort within their group.
   (ii) Each group member has a task/role/responsibility, therefore, must believe that they are responsible for their learning and that of their group.

(2) Promoting Face-to-Face Interactions:
   (i) Members promote each other's success.
   (ii) Students explain to one another what they have or are learning and assist other with understanding and completion of assignments.

(3) Individual Accountability:
   (i) Each student demonstrates master of the content being studied.
   (ii) Each student is accountable for his/her learning and work.

(4) Social Skills:
   (i) Social skills are necessary for successful cooperative learning to occur.
   (ii) Social skills include effective communication, interpersonal and group skills like leadership, decision-making, trust-building, communication and conflict-management skills.

(5) Group Processing:
   Every group must assess their effectiveness and decide how it can be improved. For student achievement, to improve considerably, two characteristics must be present:
   (i) Students are working towards a group goal or recognition, and
   (ii) Success is reliant on each individual's learning.

When designing cooperative learning tasks and reward structures, individual responsibility and accountability must be identified. Individuals must know exactly what their responsibilities are and what they are accountable to the group in order to reach their goals. Positive interdependence among students in the group for the task should be there and visible for effective learning. All group members must be involved in order for the group to complete the task. For this to occur each member must have a task that they are responsible for which cannot be completed by any other group members.

Q17. Illustrate the features, steps and uses of concept map.

Ans. The following are the features of a concept map:

    (1)   Concept map is a means by which concepts and the organisation of subject matter can be represented.

    (2)   It is a two-dimensional representation or a part of discipline (Stewart *et. al.,* 1979).

    (3)   It shows the degree of inclusiveness of the concepts.

    (4)   It is hierarchical in nature.

    (5)   It shows a pattern of concepts from general to specific.

    (6)   It shows the branching of inclusive concepts.

    (7)   It shows the cross links among concepts.

Steps in Concept Mapping: Although there are no specific steps, the following steps, suggested by J.D. Novak in his writings on concept maps, may be followed to construct a concept map:

    (1)   Select an item for mapping. This could be an important text, passage, lecture notes, or a laboratory background material.

    (2)   Choose and underlie key words or phrases; include objects and events in the list.

    (3)   Rank the list of concepts from the abstract and inclusive to the most concrete and specific.

    (4)   Cluster the concepts according to two criteria: (a) Concepts that function at a similar level of abstraction, and (b) concepts that interrelate closely.

    (5)   Link related concepts with lines and label each line in propositional form.

Uses of Concept maps: A concept map can be used at any stage of the lesson. When it is used at the introductory stage, students get a complete picture of what they are going to learn. If it is used at the developmental stage, students are taken smoothly from one concept to another. When it is used at the evaluation stage it can assess the understanding level of the students. They help in summarising whatever the learners have learnt.

Q18. What is meant by critical pedagogy? What steps are involved in it?

Ans. Teacher and student engagement is critical in the classroom because it has the power to define whose knowledge will become a part of school-related knowledge and whose voices will shape it. Students are not just young people for whom adults should devise solutions. They are critical observers of their own conditions and needs, and should be participants in discussions and problem solving related to their education and future opportunities. Hence, children need to be aware that their experiences and perceptions are important and should be encouraged to develop the mental skills needed to think and reason independently and have the courage to dissent. What children learn out of school — their capacities, learning abilities, and knowledge base — and bring to school is important to further enhance the learning process. This is all the more critical for children from underprivileged backgrounds, especially girls, as the worlds they inhabit and their realities are under-represented in school knowledge.

Critical pedagogy provides children adequate opportunities to express their views, interact and solve problems. Such process will lead to the transformation of oneself as well as of the society. Critical pedagogy is a teaching approach which attempts to help students question and challenge domination, beliefs and practices that dominate. It helps students to achieve critical consciousness.

Participatory learning and teaching, emotion and experience need to have a definite and valued place in the classroom. While class participation is a powerful strategy, it loses its pedagogic edge when it is ritualised, or merely becomes an instrument to enable teachers to meet their own ends. From the experiences of both students and teachers true participation is started.

Steps that a teacher can follow in following critical pedagogy in a class are as below:

(1) Create optimum opportunities for the students to critically analyse the issue.

(2) Announce the issue to the class and a fix a date for discussion.

(3) A teacher may also ask them to collect information regarding the issue well in advance.

(4) Students will have to actively participate when they give their view points for and against the issue and discussing the questions.

Suggested steps to be followed are illustrated below:

- **Topic:** People and Environment
- **Teaching Points:** Reasons for increased deforestation

  - Effects of deforestation

  - Ways of protecting forests
- **Issue involved:** Increased deforestation
- **Question:** Should we go for increased deforestation?

Differing view points:

- *For:* Urbanisation

  Industrialisation

  Increase food production
- *Against:* Increased pollution

  Depletion of ground water

  Imbalance in nature

  Environmental degradation

Critical questions to be discussed:

- What has made us go for deforestation?
- How can we meet the needs of growing population without deforestation?
- How will the earth be if there are no forests at all?
- How does deforestation affect human beings?
- In what ways can we protect forests?

Teacher has to help the students to collect information by telling them the sources-print, audio, visual, etc. It is not necessary to arrive at conclusion. The approach aims at creating a platform to the students to critically look at the issues prevailing in the society.

Q19. Define 'problem solving'. Also, explain its steps.

Ans. Problem-solving is one of the effective teaching-learning methods to teach social sciences at secondary level. Some are of the view problem-solving cannot be taught to learners. However, there are some higher order thinking skills like comprehension, analysis, synthesis, gereralisation, etc. which are associated with problem-solving.

Some features of problem-solving method are as follows:

(1) A felt difficulty/need to reach the goal;

(2) A goal to be reached;

(3) Reaching the goal or arriving at satisfactory solution to the problem at hand; and

(4) Challenging the felt difficulty through conscious, planned purposeful attack.

Steps: Following are the various steps, which should be involved in problem-solving:

(1) **Identifying and defining the problem:** Problem arises out of felt need and out of existing students' activities and environmental activities. The students should be able to identify and clearly define the problem.

(2) **Analysis of the problem:** The problem should be properly analysed.

(3) **Stating clearly the relationships:** It should be done between different concepts.

(4) **Formulating hypotheses:** Possible solution may be formulated basing on the nature of the problem.

(5) **Testing the hypotheses:** Each hypothesis is to be tested to solve the problem.

(6) **Verification of the result:** The solution of the problem is to be verified number of times to test the validity of the hypotheses.

Q20. What is the meaning of experiential learning? Discuss the stages involved in experiential learning.

Or

What is experiential learning? Discuss the steps involved in it that pave the way to meaningful learning.

Or

Explain the steps included in experiential Learning Cycle.

Ans. Experiential learning occurs when a person engages in some activity, looks back at the activity critically, draws some useful insight from this analysis, and puts the result to work. Learning which is developed experientially is "owned" by the learner and becomes an effective and integral aspect of behavioural change. Skill development occurs through Experiential Learning.

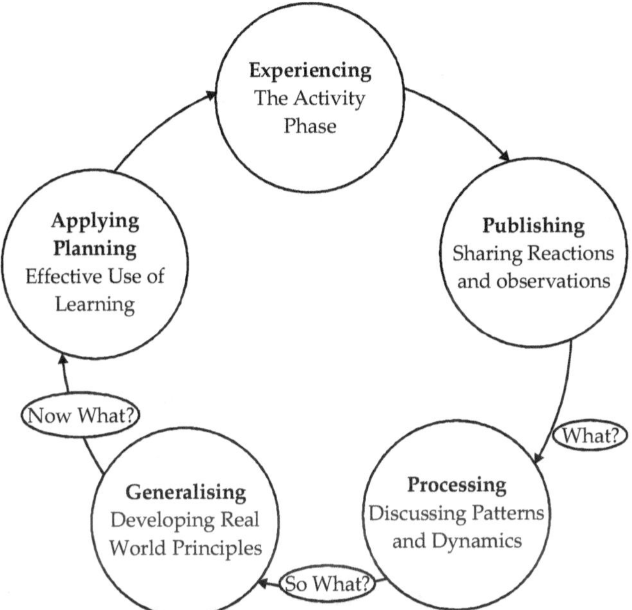

Fig. 3.1: Experiential Learning Cycle

The experiential learning cycle consists of five important stages that pave the way to meaningful learning, given as follows:

(1) **Experiencing:** The first stage of the cycle is experiencing. Almost any activity that involves self-assessment or interpersonal interaction may be used as the "doing" part of experiential learning.

(2) **Publishing:** In this second stage of the cycle, people that have experienced an activity are presumably ready to share what they saw and how they felt during the activity.

(3) **Processing:** This stage is the pivotal step in experiential learning. Group members systematically examine their common shared experience. This is the group dynamics phase of the cycle where group members essentially analyse what happened. Group members try to determine why it happened the way it did. This talking through part of the cycle is critical.

(4) Generalising: In this stage, the members of the group begin to focus on their awareness of situations in their personal or work lives that are similar to those that they experienced in the group.

(5) Applying: In this final stage, the facilitator helps participants apply generalisations to actual situations in which they are involved.

Q21. Describe about storytelling. What are its advantages and limitations?

Or

Write briefly the process of story-telling approach at upper primary level. **[April-2016, Q.No.-38]**

Ans. Children have an innate love of stories. Stories create magic and a sense of wonder at the world. Stories teach us about life, about ourselves and about others. It's no surprise that stories are still used today to improve retention and comprehension of language teaching at all levels. One of the main reasons for this is the very structure of a story: the words themselves. Through understanding of stories, children can also develop an understanding of how best to utilise language – as well as boosting their vocabulary.

Storytelling is a process. A process that involves understanding the dramatic issue or idea at the heart of a story and arranging a story's elements to bring that issue to resolution in a way that offers the story's audience a dramatic experience of fulfillment.

Storytelling, the art of narrating a tale from memory rather than reading it is one of the oldest of all art forms, reaching back to prehistoric times. Storytelling involves two elements – selection and delivery. Many teachers are interested in storytelling as a resource in teaching. A successful storyteller chooses adequate stories and must be a good performer, for the delivery is crucial and requires both preparation and rehearsal. Storytelling is the original form of teaching and has the potential of fostering emotional intelligence and help the child gain insight into human behaviour.

A teacher's capacity as an actor and speaker can make the lesson lively and interesting, to the students. They can make students almost visualize the events and the personalities concerned. To keep the listener on track, the narrator asks simple questions in between, which requires to be answered in one or two words. This method is suitable to teach social science especially History, at the elementary stage. This would arouse interest of children and provide them scope for imaginative understanding and thorough enjoyment.

Story telling can be relied upon by the teacher as the best companion for developing traits of character such as charity, piety, truthfulness, velour, etc. among students.

Advantages of Story Telling Method:
- This is a verbal presentation story.
- The attention and interest is in existence from beginning to end and the child is curious for knowing further details.

- By this method the imagination, recall and thinking power is developed.
- This method gives opportunities for showing the hidding feelings of the students.
- According to Jarvis, "This method is helpful for characteristic development and ideal formation and good qualities of the students.
- They listen the stories of great men and get inspiration.
- This method arouses interest to History in students.
- The students feel freshness.

Disadvantages of Story Telling Method:

- This is a verbal method hence success depends on the story.
- If the story is not according to the standard, the students would not interest. Hence, there would be no concentration.
- Every reference can't be taught by Story Method.
- In Storytelling Method teacher, called story and students are the listener and hence sense organs of the child are inactive.
- This method is one sided. The student can solve his problem after the end of the story.
- This method is effectless for secondary and higher secondary level.
- In this method child accepts the Teaching Method as a story but Historical, Social, Cultural and Economic aspects cannot analysed and differentiated.

Q22. Define 'field trips'. Identify steps involved in field trips.

Ans. Field trips are a way of enhancing classroom learning by making real world connections. The trips give students the opportunity to observe a particular environment that enables first-hand experience of what they are learning. In addition, students achieve a higher level of critical thinking when they evaluate their own learning compared with what they get exposed to, and they are able to modify their knowledge based on their personal experiences.

Field trips also offer students and teachers the opportunity to interact outside of the classroom, thus enhancing their bonding with each other and improving their social and life skills.

The following steps are used in organising field trips:

(1) Formulating specific objectives for the field trip.

(2) Planning and organising the activities so that the objectives can achieved effectively.

(3) Permission should be taken from school or college authority for organising field Trip.

(4) A schedule is to be prepared for the field trip (i) Date, (ii) Time, (iii) No. of students, (iv) Incharge of the field trip, (v) Specific programme for the trip, and (vi) Financial assistance.

(5) Incharge of the field trip has to contact the places or institutions for the permission as per schedule.

(6) A guideline and schedule paper is prepared for each and every students.

(7) Incharge of the trip has to prepare schedule for boarding and lodging at different places during the field Trip.

(8) A list of the required items is prepared for the journey.

(9) The specific instructions are given for the starting place and time.

(10) Incharge has to prepare code and conduct which every student has to follow during field trips.

A guide sheet is prepared and it should be checked. Every students should be well aware about the guide sheet. Every student has to full the guide sheet. The format of guide sheet should be very comprehensive and specific. Proper instructions are given for completing the guide sheet by the students.

Q23. What is discussion method? Enumerate its features and stages.

Ans. Discussion methods are a variety of forums for open-ended, collaborative exchange of ideas among a teacher and students or among students for the purpose of furthering students thinking, learning, problem solving, understanding, or literary appreciation. Participants present multiple points of view, respond to the ideas of others, and reflect on their own ideas in an effort to build their knowledge, understanding, or interpretation of the matter at hand.

The main purpose of discussion is to learn and educate individuals in the process of "group thinking" and "collective decision". Discussion is an important means of exchanging ideas with others and "often results in pooling opinions and joint action". Agreement is the declared purpose of a discussion. It is always organised and undertaken in a disciplined atmosphere.

Features of Discussion Method:

- Ensure maximum participation.
- Students have the opportunity to criticise and evaluate.
- Logical and meaningful criticism should be accepted.
- Students should anchor the discussion themselves.
- Keeping teachers as guide.
- Teacher selects the topic only with the help of students.
- Teacher divides the class in to different groups and gives the topic of the discussion to each group.
- Every group has a leader to anchor and conduct the discussion.
- Students who have leadership quality should be selected for anchoring.
- Relevant topic should only be considered.
- In the end, teacher draws the conclusion of the discussion with the help of leaders.

Organising Discussion: To make proper use of the discussion method, the teacher and student representatives should do considerable planning. In planned and well-directed procedure discussion, the whole process may be divided into three stages—preparation, discussion and evaluation.

(1) **Planning and Preparation:** Thorough preparation for the discussion is very necessary. The teacher should read wide and deep enough. He should read purposefully and critically and prepare the material conscientiously. Points to be discussed should be arranged logically. They should be written on the chalk board for guidance. The problem to be discussed should be a felt problem. If the students do not initially feel its need, they should be brought to do so.

(2) **Conduct of discussion:** While conducting the discussion, the teacher should see that it is disciplined. The arrangement of seats should ensure face-to-face talk, since the strength of the discussion is obtained from the information and viewpoint of all members of the group, it is essential that all contribute to its progress. It is a thinking-together process which breaks down if one member of the group dominates it. The teacher must see that every member of the group participates. He should encourage sincere questions and comments. The discussion must be geared to the realisation of specific objectives and development of proper skills and methods.

A relaxed and informal climate is essential if desirable results are to be achieved. The teacher should see that the discussion is truly a cooperative experience, not a competitive quarrel. He must continually discourage attack upon persons and seek to bring the participants to focus their comments on the proposition not the person. He should ensure that discussion is objective-oriented. His questions should be skilful and his direction sound. He should also see that a happy rapport is established between the teacher and the taught.

(3) **Evaluation:** Discussion must result in certain achievements such as expanding information or lessening or removing prejudices, changing attitudes or ideals, increasing the range of his interest, altering his ideas concerning national and international policies, or causing him to become a more active citizen. We must evaluate the discussion with these motives in mind.

Q24. What the meaning of map? What are its elements?

Or

Mention any *two* uses of maps.   **[April-2016, Q.No.-40]**

Ans. Maps are flat representations of the earth's surface, which convey information by means of lines, symbols, words and colours. Maps are the universally accepted symbol for the presentation of the concept of space. Every happening takes place in a definite place and in a fixed time. The place of occurrence has some influence over the course of happening, hence proper use of maps can explain adequately about the incident. Thus, a map is almost indispensable in most history lessons.

In Social Studies, the teacher has to develop the abstract concepts of time, place and distance. For their concrete representation, maps are useful means because places, boundaries, mountains rivers, directions and climate, etc. are shown with the help of lines, points and colours, etc. in the map. Maps are used not only in teaching, but they are used in many other fields also. Tourists, soldiers, scouts, boatmen, administrators and persons working in different fields must have knowledge about maps. Rudyard Kipling once said, "Intelligent participation in any discussion requires knowledge of the map of the world."

The elements of a map: The elements of a map are given below:

- **Title of the Map:** The title of a map should indicate the area represented by the map and the nature of the data displayed, as in Canada: Population, or Geology of British Columbia. In the case of data that may change over time, it also is important to specify the date of compilation, as in Energy Consumption in France, 1978 - 1982 or World Gross National Product, 1987. The most prominent lettering on a map should be reserved for the title which should be concise yet informative and well separated from the rest of the map data.
- **Direction Indicator:** This is a figure given in some corner of the map that shows the direction of the map.
- **Scale of a Map:** This is a measuring tool which is in the form of a ratio between the distance on the map and distance on the ground. This is shown either at the top or bottom of the map.
- **Colours and Symbols:** These are used in the maps which have their own meaning. Their meaning is given in a part of the map called legend. This contains the list of symbols/colours used in a given map and its meaning.

Q25. What skills are required to read maps? How these skills can be developed in students? Discuss.

Or

Define 'map scale'. **[April-2016, Q.No.-29]**

Ans. The skills required to read maps are discussed as follows:

    (1)   Noting Directions
    (2)   Recognizing Scale of a map and computing distances
    (3)   Reading Colours
    (4)   Reading Symbols
    (5)   Making Inferences by relating different maps

The above skills can be developed among the students as follows:

(1) Noting Directions: A map is always drawn in relation to direction. In part of the map, we can see the 'Direction Indicator'.

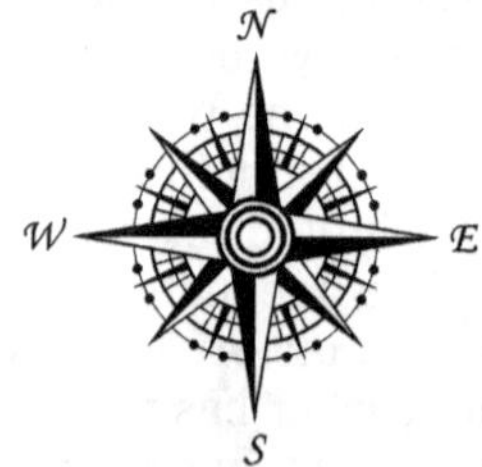

Fig. 3.2: Direction Indicator

This shows that the top of the map stands for north direction. Once we know one direction, it is possible to find out the other directions.

There are two types of directions. They are Cardinal Directions and Intermediary Directions. There are totally eight directions in which four are Cardinal. They are East, West, North and South. The four Intermediary Directions fall between the four Cardinal Directions. They are North East, North West, South East and South West.

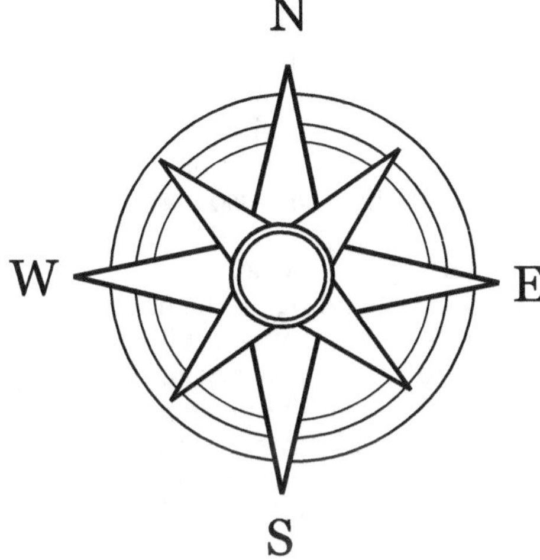

Fig. 3.3: Cardinal Directions

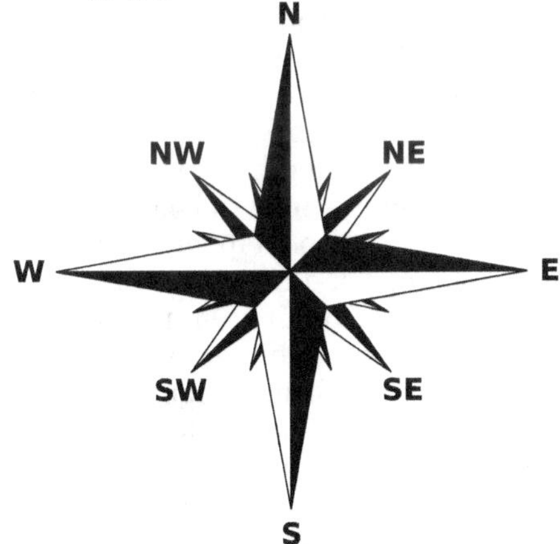

Fig. 3.4: Intermediate Directions

(2) Scale of a Map and Computing distances: Scale of a map is a measuring device. It is given in every map. Each map has its own scale. It is a ratio between the distance on a map and distance on the ground. Example 1:10,000 means one unit on the map is equal to 10,000 units on the ground. Map scale is normally expressed in following ways:

Statement form: 1cm = 100 Kms.

Representative Fraction: 1 : 10,000

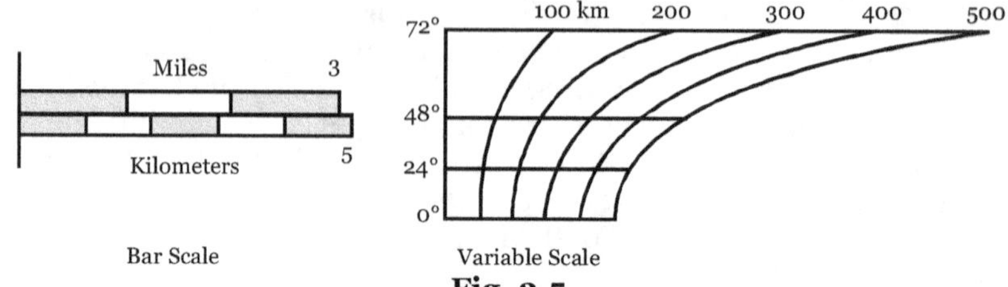

Fig. 3.5

Graphic on scale: With the help of scale of a map, one can measure the distance between the places, length of a river or a coast line, etc.

Students can find the approximate distance/length by computing themselves by learning how to use scale of a map. This increases the interest of the students and they can also play with the maps, using Atlas in groups during free time in computing the distance. This will increase the skill of the students in using Map Scale.

(3) Reading Colours: Depending on the nature/theme of a map, colours used on a map have different meanings. If it is a political map, the colours indicate different political units. If it is a physical map, the colours stand for the height of the land above the mean sea level or the depth of water below the mean sea level. In physical map, certain colours are conventionally used and they have universally accepted meaning. Example: Shades of green stand for low land, wherein, darker the green lower the height of the low land from the mean sea level.

Here, we can make out the actual height of a given land or depth of the water body. This is understood by using an element of a map called Legend. Legend or Index / Key is found in every map wherever colours are used. This is a small rectangular box drawn on a map with tiny coloured boxes. There will be different shades of colours. Each shaded tiny box stands for the range of height or depth as indicated against it.

We can understand the meaning of colours used in the given map by reading the legend. We can also help our learners to develop skill in reading colours by using maps of different themes with colours.

(4) Reading Map Symbols: In different maps, the information is shown in different forms. It is shown through colours or symbols whichever is appropriate. Symbols are in the form of figures/letters. They represent the resources of the earth on a map. Only when we are able to understand what these symbols mean, we can get information from the maps.

The conventional and non-conventional are two types of symbols. The conventional symbols have universally accepted meanings and have been in use for a very long time. Whereas, the non- conventional symbols are used by the map maker according to her/his choice. Once we develop the skill of reading colours and symbols of a map, we will be in a position to understand the map better.

(5) Making Inferences by relating different maps: It is very easy to draw inference after we develop the skills of Noting directions, Recognising Scale of a map and computing distances, Reading Colours and Reading Symbols. Inference is conclusion reached or judgments arrived at by reasoning from data/ observation/ facts at hand. It suggests indirectly that something is true.

For example, if we have to study about growing of coffee, take the crops map of India, we identify the places where coffee is grown in India taking the help of legend. We look into physical map of India and identify the land forms of those places where coffee is grown. We look into the climate map, soil map, rainfall map, population map, etc. and find out what conditions have favoured the growing of coffee in those places. We can even predict a place where coffee can be grown. This is how we make inferences based on several observations from one map or/ and based on several observations from more than one map.

Q26.Explain the concept, need and importance of learning resources in the teaching-learning process of social sciences.

Ans. The things, which can be used to achieve an aim, are called resources. Learning resources are the materials that are used for teaching a course. A teacher uses a number of resources like a dictionary, a map or a model etc. to help himself transact lessons better. It can be understood better with the help of following examples:

- A teacher willing to teach about plants may use the school garden as a learning resource.
- To clarify the concept of river and pond, the teacher may arrange a visit to a river or pond or s/he can show a video-clip or a picture of it.

In teaching learning process of social sciences we tend to use various objects, materials, people, and buildings to transact the content. Some of these learning resources are referred to as Instructional Aids/Instructional Media. There is a wealth of learning resources which can be used in teaching of social sciences. We are familiar with common learning resources such as blackboard (chalkboard), charts, models, video film, radio, etc.

The resources may be used by teachers, students or both during instruction so as to maximise the attainment of instructional objectives.

The importance of learning resources is stressed in Focus Group Paper of Teaching of Social Sciences as follows: 'Teaching should utilise greater resources of audio-visual materials, including photographs, charts and maps and replicas of archaeological and materials cultures'.

The following points explain the need and importance of learning resources in teaching-learning process:

- Learning resources help the learners achieve the learning objectives more effectively and efficiently.
- Application of these learning resources makes teaching and learning effective.
- They also have the capacity to provide real (direct) or almost real experiences.
- Some of these resources are used to create readiness in the learners for acquiring learning experiences.

- Learning resources help in clarifying, interpreting and appreciating concepts. They provide clarity, precision and accuracy in processing information.
- They create visual images, which help retention of the learnt concepts. Some of them also provide stimulation to more than one sense (e.g. video film or television)
- They help students learn faster, remember longer, gain more accurate information.
- Some resources provide the learners opportunity to learn individually at their own pace (e.g. computer-assisted instructional programme, or in a small group (models, assignments, newspaper cuttings for discussion, etc.), or in a large group (e.g. 35 m.m. film or slides).

Q27. What are realia and diorama? How to procure realia and construct diorama?

Or

What is the meaning of 'Diorama'?   [April-2016, Q.No.-27]

Ans. Realia: The term "realia" refers to real objects such as tools, utensils, art objects, clothing, etc., that are made and used by people in a given culture or society (Ord, 1972). For example, while teaching tools used in agriculture, the teacher can collect some tools used by the people in agriculture and show these to the students. Sometimes, a teacher can organize a trip to a nearby museum and show to the student ornaments, arms and weapons, utensils, etc. used by the people in the past.

How to procure Realia?

One can collect samples of rocks, soils, mineral resources while conducting field trips.

We can procure them from the community or they can be hired from museums.

Teaching with the help of Realia creates a lot of interest among the students as they are always fascinated by real things than created ones. While teaching chapter on resources we may use specimens of soils, rocks, minerals, agricultural products. While teaching political history one can make use of coins, jewelry, dresses, etc. While teaching chapter on agriculture, samples of various crops can be used to provide them real experience.

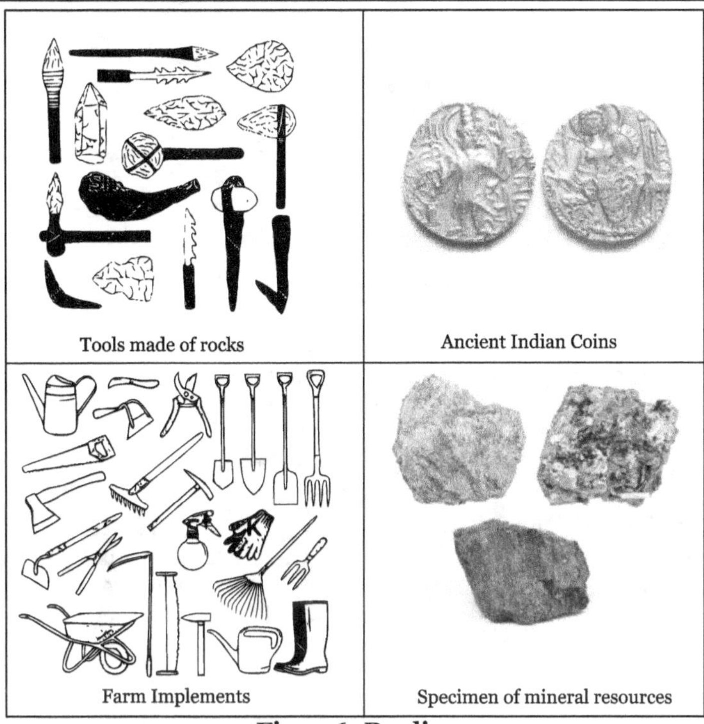

Tools made of rocks	Ancient Indian Coins
Farm Implements	Specimen of mineral resources

Fig. 3.6: Realia

Diorama: A diorama is a three-dimensional scene which depicts a basic human activity or way of life typical of a given culture or people (Ord, 1972). Adiorama can be prepared by taking a medium-sized pasteboard box with one end cut out. The background scenes are painted on paper which is pasted to the sides and at the back of the box on the inside surfaces. The landscapes, humans, figures, trees, etc., are made by paper sculpting and are connected to the floor so as to stand, thus giving a three-dimensional effect. This can be a powerful teaching aid of social sciences for depicting the actual life in a given society at a particular point of time.

How to construct Diorama?

There are many things like cardboard, thermocol sheets, clay, readymade synthetic materials like plants, bushes, shrubs, etc. from diorama can be constructed.

In most of the Geography textbook, there is ample scope of using diorama. For example, Diorama can be constructed for depicting Life in Deserts, Oasis in the Sahara desert and life in cold desert, etc. Beautiful diorama can also be prepared for Paddy cultivation in Brahmaputra valley and tea gardens in Assam. Diorama can also be prepared for depicting natural vegetation and wildlife.

Life in Desert   Life in Polar Areas

Fig. 3.7: Diorama

Since at this stage children learn more through observation, it is necessary to use diorama to have a feeling of life of people in a particular geographical region.

Q28. Briefly describe about maps and globs.

Or

Define the term 'Globe'.   **[April-2016, Q.No.-26]**

Ans. All of us use maps in one form or the other in our daily life. When we tour a new place, we take the help of maps. Thus, maps represent the earth or parts of the earth upon a flat surface. The earth is represented on the map through lines, dots, colours, words and signs. In social sciences, maps are very important for learning many geographical, historical and economic concepts.

Globes are a scale model of the earth in three dimensions. These are the only kind of map that can give pupils a true conception of geographical relationships.

Maps provide more information than a globe. Maps are of different types. Maps showing natural features of the earth such as mountains, plateaus, plains, rivers, oceans etc. are called physical or relief maps. Maps showing cities, towns and villages and different countries and states of the world with their boundaries are called political maps. Some maps focus on specific information such as showing distribution of temperature, rainfall, forests, minerals, industries, population, transportation, etc. These are known as thematic maps. Maps help in understanding in learning concepts, help in synthesising and integrating ideas and help to draw reasonable inferences and observations.

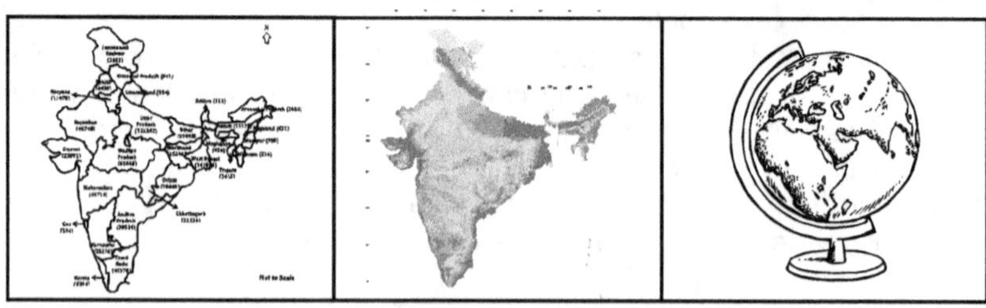

(a) India: Political Map   (b) India: Physical Map   (c) Globe

Fig. 3.8: Types of maps and globes

Q29. What is meant by 'models'? Enlist their three types.

Ans. Models are three-dimensional visual aids. They represent real things in all respects except size and shape. Large objects are reduced to small size so that they could be observed by students with greater precision. Models may be simple (static), sectional or working. Simple models like deities worshiped by the people of the Indus Valley Civilisation could be prepared and shown to the students. In a sectional model of the earth, for example, all parts of the earth can be separated, shown to the students and replaced.

Working models are used to show the actual operation or working of a real object. A working model of the Continental Ocean Currents would show how actually currents flow in different oceans of the world.

A variety of models can be prepared for illustrating various contents of social studies. Some examples of models in social sciences are as follows:

- Models of historical architecture and sculpture.
- Models of solar system or wind mills.

Models are generally prepared using materials like cardboard paper, wood, bamboo, thermocol, wax, plaster of Paris, plastics, metals, clay, strings, etc.

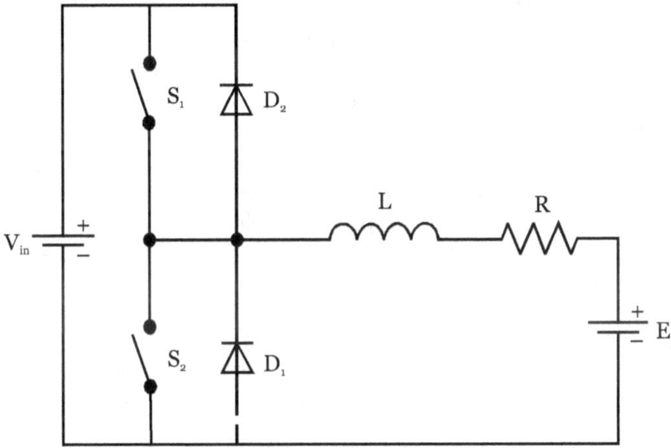

Fig. 3.9: Static Model

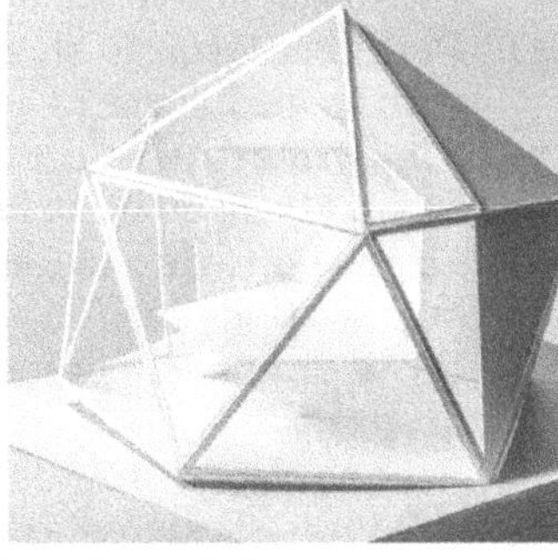

Fig. 3.10: Sectional Model

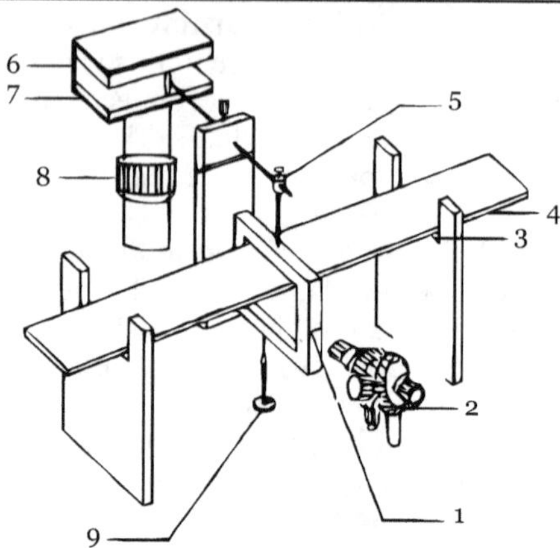

Fig. 3.11: Working Model

Q30. Define charts, graphs and cartoons.

Or

Enumerate the types of charts.

Or

What are organization charts?   **[October-2016, Q.No.-38]**

Ans. Charts: Charts are a valuable tool for use in social studies. A chart is a simple flat pictorial display material and, if used appropriately, conveys the displayed information in a highly effective manner. Charts serve as an excellent means of classifying important information that is to be referred to a number of times. They help summarise and simplify complex ideas which students face during reading. Jarolimek (1967) classifies charts under two basic headings, Formal and Informal. Formal charts include the following kinds:

(1) **Narration charts** portray historical developments or depict steps in a procedure, such as how a bill becomes law.

(2) **Tabulation charts** present data in the form of table in order to facilitate making comparisons.

(3) **Relationship charts** show cause-and-effect relationships such as factors related to the pollution of the environment.

(4) **Pedigree charts** show development that have a single origin such as the lineage of a family.

(5) **Classification charts** point out various kinds of relations such as those in basic food charts.

(6) **Organisation charts** show the internal structure of organizations such as a corporation or governmental bodies.

(7) **Flow charts** show steps in a process such as the manufacture of steel.

Information charts are developed by the teacher and students throughout a unit of study as a means of developing standards or summaries of materials related to the ongoing study.

Frequency of Performances of Shakespeare's Plays 1755-1765			
Genre	**Number of Plays**	**Number of Performances**	**Average per Play**
Histories	6	247	41.2
Tragedies	8	328	41
Romances	3	112	37
Comedies	9	161	18
Total	26	848	32.6

Fig. 3.12: Tabulation Chart

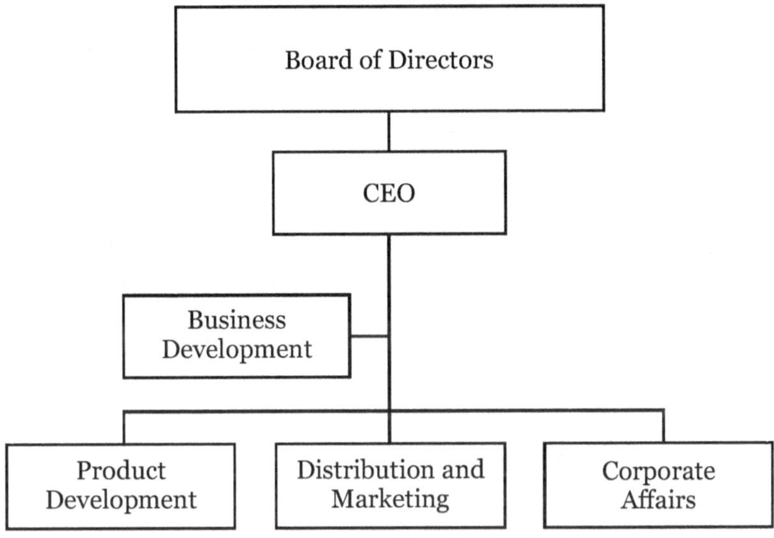

Fig. 3.13: Organization Chart

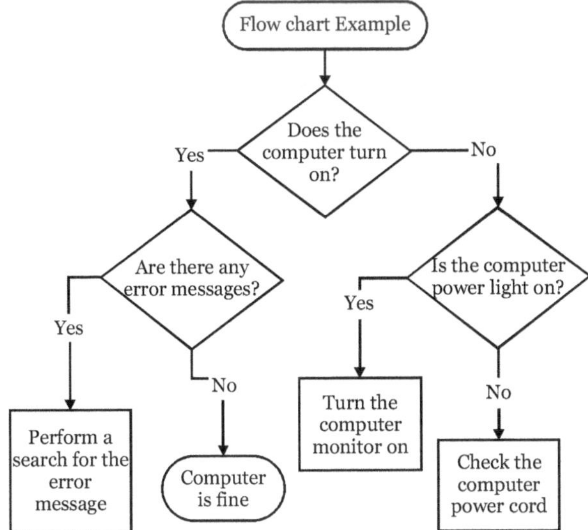

Fig. 3.14: Flow chart

Graphs: Graphs are used to present numerical figures or statistical data. Numerical data is shown through lines, dots and figures. For example, if we have to show the relative position of supply and demand of the year or month wise, graphs can be powerful medium. Graph not only introduces activity into the teaching-learning process, but also provides training to students to present the facts or time period through the use of lines, numbers, dots, etc. Graphs help in presenting the abstract ideas through visual bars or images. Graphs are powerful and effective means of presenting the analysis of facts or comparative studies with the help of numbers, figures or bars. No other medium can present facts in this way. Again, if the extensive content is to be presented in brief, graph can be very effective. Graphs can be studied quickly and can also be used for ready reference.

Graphs are mainly of four types:

    (1)   Picture Graph
    (2)   Bar Graph
    (3)   Line Graph
    (4)   Circle Graph

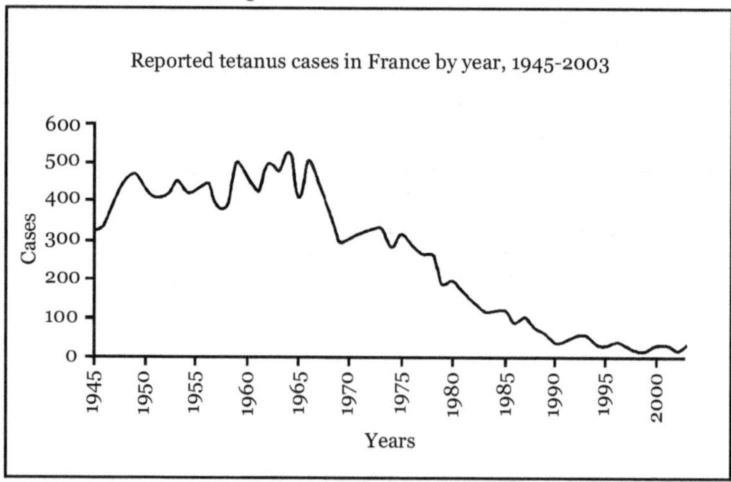

Fig. 3.15: Line Graph

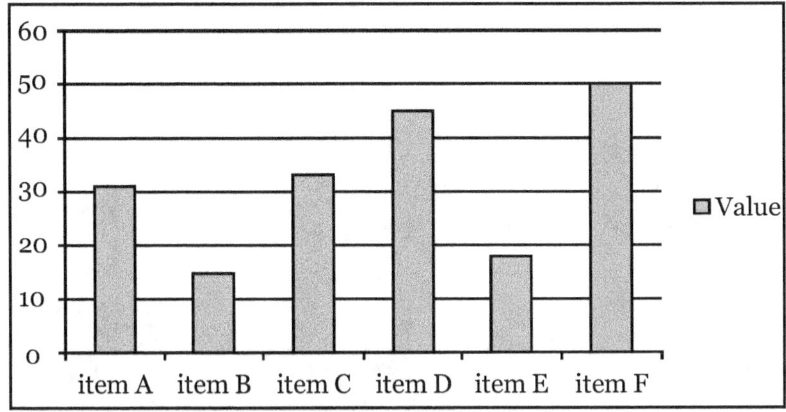

Fig. 3.16: Bar Graph

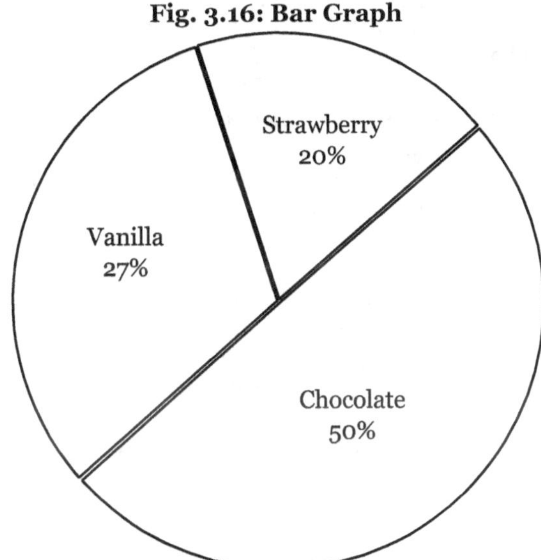

Fig. 3.17: Pie Graph

Cartoons: These days social sciences textbooks based on NCF 2005 contains lots of graphics, pictures and cartoons. Use of cartoons as learning resources brings visual relief and some fun. Cartoons carry lot of message and students also learn to interpret their messages. A teacher must collect cartoons from regional languages and use them frequently in his/her classrooms. Sometimes these cartoons give us the space to take a detour and get into a side discussion that is often richer than the main one. One can give assignments to students on these cartoons.

Fig. 3.18: Cartoons

Q31. Explain in brief about time-lines.

Or

Explain two uses of time lines in teaching historical aspects of Social Science.   **[October-2016, Q.No.-39]**

Ans. Time lines are very simple devices which reduce time sense into space sense for easy comprehension. It helps in knowing 'how much before' and 'how much after' of an event. The concept of space also involves the concept of sequence of distance. Time is represented by a horizontal or vertical line and happenings are fixed on it according to their dates of occurrence in a chronological sequence.

Time lines can be of different kinds-Progressive and regressive time lines, pictorial time lines and comparative time lines etc.

In progressive time lines, the sequence of happenings march from the past of the present as the happenings have actually occurred in time. In regressive time lines, the sequence of happenings march from present to the past, as if we were moving backward.

Progressive time lines present the happenings in a chronological sequence on a horizontal or vertical lines. A line is divided into actual units comprising an inch or half inch, etc.

When we try to give to the child and idea about the happening of an event, we tell him that it occurred before his birth, his father's and grandfather's and even much earlier than that, regressive time line is helpful. It develops in pupils their first sense of time sequence is regard to historical events. Such time lines are of a great use for primary classes.

Time lines can be made pictorial to make them attractive. The events or personalities to be located on the time line, may be presented through picture symbols.

Q32. Define 'books'. What are its types?

Ans. A book is a series of pages assembled for easy portability and reading, as well as the composition contained in it. Following are the types of books:

   (1)   **Textbooks:** A textbook is a manual of instruction in any branch of study. Textbooks are produced according to the demands of educational institutions. In other words, textbooks are seen as indispensable source of knowledge usually prescribed either by the government or govt. authorised examining agency. At the national level, textbooks are brought by the NCERT, whereas at the state level we have state text bureaus or SCERT for development of textbooks. It is essential that course related standard textbooks, frequently referred to and used during training, are always available with the students and teachers. For instructional process minimum requirement is textbooks. To ensure this, some copies of textbooks should be kept in the reference section.

(2) **Reference books and manuals:** These are usually expensive resources which the learners refer to during instructional process. Normally, two or three copies of each volume are kept in the school library according to the users' likely demand. These books and manuals must not be taken out of the resource centre. These supplementary books can be subject specific dictionaries, atlases, encyclopaedias, yearbooks, statistical abstracts, government reports, magazines and journals, manuscripts, general books, review books. In order to promote creativity, aesthetics and critical perspectives, wider depth of understanding of concepts, there must be supplementary books for learning social sciences.

    (i)   School Atlas

    (ii)   Administrative Atlas of India

(3) **Periodicals, technical and professional magazines and journals:** These are instructional sources, which learners refer to for state-of-the-art information. Though quite expensive, these are of much use to both teachers and learners. Normally, these are not issued on loan to users.

(4) **Collections:** We can also assemble many current materials for our own use and for the use of students. These consist of a variety of materials, sometimes retained under subject headings and sometimes kept loose. Collections include newspaper cuttings, cut-out articles from magazines and commercially bought information packs, photographs, extracts from the work of previous learners, diagrams, graphs, and other types of written and graphic materials. Collections can be made both by the staff as well as by the learners and they (the learners) should be encouraged to collect and develop banks of resource materials.

(5) **Instructional materials:** These include self-instructional materials because learners can use them independently during the process of instruction. Various types of self-instructional materials are available in the market. These are programmed learning texts, semi-programmed learning modules, capsules, etc.

Q33. Why and how we use newspapers clippings in the study of social sciences?

Ans. Through social sciences, we develop the learner's critical understanding about the society and its dimensions like polity and economy. These dimensions are highly dynamic. Textbooks though a good source of knowledge may not keep good pace with the ever changing society as they are written after a long gap and regular revised editions are difficult to bring out in short span of time. Thus, newspapers which carry reporting of day-to-day events like polity, economy, natural disasters, etc.

Social science teacher should keep abreast of current events by reading a variety of newspapers. It is important to read newspapers which represent various points of view on current and controversial issues.

There are several ways in which teacher can use newspapers:

- Preparation of files on specific themes.
- Introducing the topic in the classroom.
- Use as bulletin board.
- Use in group discussions, preparation of assignments and individual study.

Q34. What do you understand by museum? How is it useful in studying social science?

Ans. A museum is an institution that cares for (conserves) a collection of artifacts and other objects of artistic, cultural, historical, or scientific importance. Many public museums make these items available for public viewing through exhibits that may be permanent or temporary. The largest museums are located in major cities throughout the world, while thousands of local museums exist in smaller cities, towns and rural areas.

Museums play a great part in the education of school children as they bring home to them much more vividly than any prosaic lectures, the discoveries of the past and the various developments that have taken place in many fields of science and technology.

Organisation of social science museum can be taken up as a co-curricular activity. Museums have great educative value. These are recreation centers also. These contain non-reading materials which represents valuable information concerning the past periods. Events, persons, etc. are presented in the form of real objects, pictures, drawings etc. The museums can procure and maintain various materials that could be effectively used in class room teaching. These can be collected, classified, and exhibited by students and teachers. It provides insight in to how people lived, how society has progressed and how science has developed since time immemorial. It stimulates enthusiasm for deep study and research among students as well as teachers.

The schools should have their own social science museums. During the summer break, students may be asked to make models of historical monuments, charts indicating the effect of volcanoes or earthquakes, crosswords games or puzzles. The children may paint phenomena related to the natural environment. Newspapers or magazines cutting related to topics in the syllabus, or related information downloaded from Internet can be displayed.

Social Science Museums play important role in the intellectual and cultural growth of students. They enrich the experiences of students. Students get the opportunity to relate what they have studied in their textbooks and classrooms which help in strengthening their knowledge and enriching their experiences. The purpose of museums is not merely to present visual aids but also to stimulate the sense of curiosity, beauty and its appreciation, spirit of inquiry of nature and natural phenomena.

Q35. What is the role of movies in teaching-learning?

Ans. Movies play the role of an interesting and effective teaching- learning aid. They can be used to explain certain concepts to the students and to communicate several vital messages. Certain movies are of great educational value as they are able to present significant information in a creative and interesting manner.

Educational movies can be obtained from Central Institutes of Educational Technology, State Institute of Educational Technology, Embassies of various countries, Ministry of Tourism and Culture, state tourism departments. Apart from that, there are many private partners; NGO's those who produce wide variety of movies for use as instructional inputs. The commercial and art cinema reflect on people life along with beautiful presentation of various landscapes and geographical areas. One can easily watch geographical features like mountains, plains, deserts, rivers, oceans, seas, islands and beaches. Teacher can either show clippings of these movies or even sometimes can show the entire film based on the learning objectives. Movies like Ambedkar by Jabbar Patel, Gandhi by Richard Attenborough, Netaji Subhas Chandra Bose by Shyam Benegal, Sardar Patel by Ketan Mehta, The Legend of Bhagat Singh by Rajkumar Santoshi are good source of knowledge with entertainment.

Q36. How do you learn social science from Internet?

Or

Write any *one* use of Internet.   [April-2016, Q.No.-28]

Ans. Internet is one of the most important source through which an individual can easily get information, remain in touch with their beloved ones, and perform thousands of activities. Moreover, the internet utilisation is vital because it is the biggest source of all aspect. However, internet covers numerous issues and developments that take place all over the world. One of the core advantages of internet is that it gives loads of data to us. Students could even utilise the internet as a substitution of reading material and reference books as it contains an endless source of learning.

For example, for teaching the chapter on Indian Monsoon, additional information can be obtained from different sources. One of the most dependable and authentic source is Indian Meteorological Department (IMD). One can access the site www.imd.ernet.in/main_new.htm and download daily weather map, satellite images of every date. Besides this the site also provides information on seismological data, seasonal or annual rainfall maps etc.

The NCERT textbooks based on NCF-2005 had also listed various websites which can be of great help to the teachers and students in probing more and learning effectively.

Directory of Indian Government Websites:
http://goidirectory.nic.in
http://presidentofindia.nic.in
http://pmindia.nic.in
http://rajyasabha.gov.in
http://loksabha.nic.in
http://supremecourtofindia.nic.in
http://eci.nic.in (Election Commission of India)
http:// sci.edu/public.html
http://volcanoes.usgs.gov
http://nationalgeographic.com
http:// school.discovery.com
http://incredibleindia.org
http:// Wikipedia.org
http://britannica.com
http://animalplanet.co.uk
http://freefoto.com
http://mnes.nic.in

Q37. Discuss school and community as learning resources of social science.

Ans. School and community can be used as learning resources in teaching learning process of social sciences. In school set up, students and teacher can be effective resources. And each person living in the neighbouring community can be a resource for learning.

(1) **Teacher as a Resource:** Teachers are themselves important instructional resources. As most of the classroom activities are controlled by the teacher, their knowledge, skills, experiences and competencies decide, to a large extent, the effectiveness of teaching-learning process. We further agree that the teacher as an individual is unique. They get experiences of teaching different individuals from various socio-economic backgrounds. A teacher must enrich her/his intellectual resources from time to time. For this, s/he has to attend national seminars, conferences, symposia, etc., to update her/his knowledge and skills.

(2) **Student as a Resource:** In making instruction joyful, interesting, useful and effective, a student can play a very important role. Through experience, teachers know that the majority of social science classrooms are boring. Students do not take part in instructional activities. They remain silent spectators. They do not ask questions even if they are unable to understand. If this trend is reversed and students are involved actively in the instructional process as it is not explained, teaching-learning can be made effective as well as a rewarding experience. In a classroom, there are students with varied personalities, socioeconomic backgrounds and intellectual abilities. All of them also have varieties of experiences. If all these are explored and integrated into the teacher's teaching, teaching certainly becomes very effective. Not only that, instruction becomes lively and students take a lot of interest in the instructional process. Students can also be helpful in producing different types of material resources as part of their project work, assignments or field work.

(3) Community as resource: For classroom learning experience, community can be utilized as supplements. A teacher must get acquainted with the community. S/he should try to have information about the physical environment, the people and their socio-economic and cultural backgrounds, religious groups in the community and their influence, their economic activities, enlightened personalities in that community and the local history of that community, places of recreation, worship, public utility, attitude of the community towards education and political set up of the community.

Community resources vary from community to community. The opportunities which the teacher in an open rural area has are only slightly related to those of teacher in an urban area. But community study opportunities are available to every school and should be explored. As we contemplate the many sources of information that are open to investigation, we must no longer overlook those, which lie within "walking distance". The local factory, retail shop, business offices are real facts school children can see, hear, ask questions about them and examine them minutely. Opined that it is the responsibility of the teacher to investigate the community, particularly those resources, which seem to identify themselves with clear-cut full understanding of social experience. Resources which include factories, health institutions, culture, infrastructure business office religion institution, to mention a little are a veritable source of course content and experiences.

Q38. Enumerate suggestions for making best use of limited resources to learn social sciences.

Ans. In order to make social sciences interesting and for better understanding of concepts social science teacher needs to use a variety of resources. But at the same time due to meagre budget allocation allotted for purchase of material in social sciences it becomes really a challenge for teachers to sustain the interest of students in the subject. In such case, one should not be disheartened. Following are certain suggestions for making best use of limited resources:

- We can use pictures of old magazines for preparing collage.
- In case school is in possession of computer with internet facilities much useful content pictures can be downloaded. We can have access to various open educational resources (OERs).

- Text books and review books often have charts and diagrams that can be used or modified; often they can be enlarged by students.
- We can save the pictures from old calendar especially carrying pictures of extinct wildlife, government initiatives and plans.
- We can procure inexpensive material free of cost from certain government agencies.
- We can compile the list of students from higher class, teachers, parents, and other adults in the community who can be used as resources in our classes.
- We may consult institutes of education and training colleges. As part of their course student teachers are supposed to prepare learning aids. Small request from our side will fetch us many learning aids.
- Start a collection of clippings from daily newspapers and preserve them as files.
- We can use waste material like cardboard, thermocol sheets, mud, plaster of paris for making models and dioramas.
- Through school administration, we can also approach parent teacher association.
- We can also borrow from, share material resources in cluster schools.
- We can assign Project work to students. Scrapbooks generated out of project work can be used in instructional process.
- Exploring resources from the community, we can invite learned people for narrating oral history, and also to share their narratives related to content we are teaching.
- We can enlarge maps on white cloth. Enlargement can be done with the help of slide projector.

Q39. What do marks indicate in assessment?

Ans. We understand about marks in assessment by following example:

In a school, 40 children of class VIII who appeared half yearly examination, scored between 20 and 95, out of 100, in social science. Majority scored between 50 and 60. Rahul, who stood first obtained 95 marks whereas Suman who stood second scored 91. Suman's mother managed to learn about the marks obtained by Rahul in different subjects and compared with that of her daughter in the progress card. She found that Suman has scored higher marks in rest of the subjects and in aggregate as well. Suman's total marks in this examination remained highest in the class. Despite all these, her mother did not express her satisfaction with the performance of Suman, the reason being she scored less in social science, particularly than Rahul, who happened to remain in second position in last many examinations. She warned Suman to see that Rahul never exceeds in any subject in the annual examination. Interestingly, the class teacher compared the marks of the two students and threw a comment on Suman's marks saying "A drop of Kerosene in a bucket of water". Suman's classmates reacted to her marks in comparison to that of Rahul in similar manner.

Many a times we must have come across the situation like this. The situation obviously indicates that this type of evaluation causes feeling of insecurity, stress, anxiety and humiliation in children as in Suman's case, even though she has scored more than 90% of marks. It brings out what the child does not know or cannot rather than what the child knows or can do. It also focuses on assessing the content knowledge acquired by rote memorisation. Most of the time, it leads to comparison and unhealthy competitions among children; and in some cases it leads to suicide even for one mark that determines position/division or pass/fail.

Q40. What are the purposes of assessment? Also enlist those purposes which are not to be assessed.

Or

Suggest any *two* objectives of assessment of learner.

[April-2016, Q.No.-39]

Or

Write any one purpose of assessment of children.

[October-2016, Q.No.-30]

Ans. Assessment is an important part of every teaching-learning process. The purpose of assessment is not only to carry out assessment of learning but also to focus on 'assessment for learning'. Assessment needs to be an integral part of teaching learning process and a tool for continuous enhancement of student learning. Of course, this is a challenge for teacher. Again, the primary objective of assessment is to ensure that the learning objectives formulated by her/him are achieved through appropriate assessment methods.

Since we are concerned about children's learning; and the purpose of assessment is to improve and gauge their learning, we must be aware of some of the reasons as to why assessment of children be made.

Following are some of the important purposes of assessment:

- To identify the individual needs and requirements.
- To improve teaching learning process.
- To find out what learning and change take place in the child over a period of time.
- To encourage and support children to learn together.
- To help the child understand about what s/he knows or can do.
- To communicate the children's progress in the subject to parents.
- To plan teaching-learning process in a more suitable way.
- To do away with the fear of assessment among children.
- To find out the extent to which the objectives of the syllabi have been achieved.

The purpose of assessment is not to:

- identify what the child does not know or cannot do.
- diagnose learning difficulties and problem areas.
- encourage children to get position (first/second) in exams.
- label children as slow learners, or bright students or 'problem children'.

- encourage children to compete with each other for marks.
- identify children who need remediation.
- help children to score more marks in exams.

Q41. What should be assessed? Also, explain some activities of children that need to considerate in the context of assessment.

Ans. Assessment is an integral part of instruction, as it determines whether or not the goals of education are being met. Assessment affects decisions about grades, placement, advancement, instructional needs, curriculum, and, in some cases, funding

Today, objective of education is to prepare the children for a meaningful and productive life, and therefore, is concerned with the all-round development of the child-physical, social, emotional, cognitive and moral. The school should support and encourage all-round or holistic development of children. All aspects need to be assessed rather than only academic achievement. Unfortunately, the current processes of evaluation, which assess a very limited range of abilities, do not provide a complete picture of an individual's abilities or progress. It is, therefore, important that assessment be undertaken for all the activities that the child participates in both inside and outside the school/classroom.

Some activities of children that need to be taken into consideration in the context of assessment are given below:

- Children's learning in subject areas.
- Children's skills, interests, attitudes and motivation.
- Children's participation in social activities.
- Children's responses to different situations and or opportunities both in and out of school.
- Children's participation in co-curricular activities.

Q42. When should assessment be done? Briefly discuss.

Ans. Assessments must clearly match the content, the nature of thinking, and the skills taught in a class. Through feedback from instructors, students become aware of their strengths and challenges with respect to course learning outcomes. There are many teachers who think that assessment of learning outcomes should go along with the teaching-learning process in a continues manner, while some resist it saying that continuous assessment reduce learning time and, therefore, is a waste of time.

There are many reasons to prefer the former view on assessment of learning outcomes. A good evaluation can become an integral part of the learning process and benefit both learners themselves and teachers by giving feedback. It is obvious that teachers use to observe the progress of their children regularly on informal basis. These informal observations no doubt, have immense implications for improving teaching–learning process and thereby children's learning. There is, however, need for some periodicity in evaluation to help teachers reflect upon the information collected about learners. Thus, assessment should be on daily basis as well as periodic.

Continuous assessment implies maintaining a profile for each child. This is required to reflect upon, derive feedback, plan and implement measures so as to enhance children's learning. Thus, continuous assessment implies a cycle of learning and assessment.

Q43. How should assessment be done? Enlist its steps.

Ans. Assessment of student learning is never completed. We continually make decisions about programs, teaching and services. So we need to collect, analyze and review information regularly. Following steps are followed in assessment process:

(1) **Collecting information about children:** Assessment is any systematic procedure for collecting information that can be used to make inferences about the characteristics of people or objects (AERA et al., 1999; Reported in Reynolds et al. 2009, p.3). In the context of collection of information about children's learning and progress, two things are important – first, to collect information from a variety of sources, and secondly, to use different methods or tools and techniques.

In most schools, it has been observed that the teacher is the primary source of information. The other important sources include:

(i) Children themselves

(ii) Parents

(iii) Child's friends / Peers/ Classmates

(iv) Community Members

(v) Principal/ Headmaster

(vi) School records (attendance register, etc.)

The most commonly used methods of collecting information are: class tests, assignments, paper–pencil tests, written and oral tests, questions on pictures, discussion with students. No single tool/technique or method can provide all the required information about a child's learning and/or progress. They can be used in different times depending on what is being assessed.

(2) **Recording of information:** Recording the information through the use of report cards is the most common form. Most report cards in schools across the country carry information in the form of marks or grades obtained by children in tests/exams. Such report cards fail to provide a complete picture of the child's learning and progress. The scope needs to be widened. Recording needs to include records of observations and comments on children's performance on assignments, ratings of what children do and how they behave and anecdotes or incidents of children's behavior towards others.

Effective Recording:

(i) Recording the observations immediately in a diary

(ii) Assessing the child's work during an activity

(iii) Writing descriptive statements of a child's work

(iv) Preparing a child's profile

    (v)   Keeping sample of a child's work in a portfolio

    (vi) Making note of important changes,

    (vii) Clarifying doubts of the child while recording

(3) **Interpretation of gathered information:** Interpretation of gathered information helps to understand and draw conclusions about the child—where the child is and what needs to be done to help the child. This requires daily analysis and review of records as well as provides reflection of collected information.

Information which is collected should not stop with collection of information/evidences. We need to carry this further with brief qualitative remarks. It is often seen that a child's response is marked with "O" or "X" or "A" or "B", etc. It is necessary to go beyond marking or grading. It means that marks or grades should be explained further. This will help in understanding why the child has done whatever s/he has attempted to do.

Q44. Why does conventional schooling less supportive for the development of a child's personality? Also, enumerate some of the major initiatives in context of assessment process.

Ans. Conventional schooling has been heavily criticised on grounds that it favours rote learning and reaps limited cognitive growth of children sidelining the socio-personal qualities. Examinations take children further from life than from books. Learners' assessment largely focuses on achievement in core subject areas only ignoring other aspects of children's life, e.g. social, emotional, physical, personal. Report cards display more the weaknesses of children than their strengths. Children's poor performance is attributed to their cognitive capacities but not to the schooling process and/or assessment approaches. Thus, the conventional examination practices were less supportive to all round development of a child's personality.

Some of the major initiatives: recommendations, policies, frameworks and Acts etc., are as follows:

    (1)   The Education Commission (1964-66) pointed out that evaluation is a continuous process and forms an integral part of the total system of education, and is intimately related to educational objectives. Hence, techniques of evaluation should be valid, reliable, objective and practical and should follow varieties of techniques while assessing learners.

    (2)   National Policy on Education (1986) envisages the need for Continuous and Comprehensive Evaluation (CCE) at all stages of school education that incorporates both scholastic and non-scholastic aspects of education, spread over the total span of instructional time.

    (3)   Programme of Action (1992) also reiterated the concept of CCE and called for preparation of a National Examination Reform Framework to serve as a set of guidelines to the examining bodies which would give the freedom to innovate and adopt the framework to suit the specific situation.

(4) National Curriculum Framework (2005) recommends continuous and comprehensive assessment and suggests flexibility in the assessment procedures at the school stages; and emphasized the assessment tasks for the learners.

(5) RTE Act (2009) has made the use of CCE mandatory till elementary stage of education. Section 29 (1) states that curriculum and evaluation procedure shall make the child free from fear, trauma and anxiety by adopting CCE; and section 3 (1) highlights that no child shall be required to pass any Board examination till completion of elementary education. Hence, need to have a functional CCE scheme for schools.

Q45.Discuss briefly the concept and objectives of Continuous and Comprehensive Evaluation (CCE).

Or

What is CCE? Discuss its need and features.

Ans. Continuous and Comprehensive Evaluation (CCE) can be defined as a process of ensuring learning performance of students through both formative and summative evaluation in different areas such as cognitive, affective and psychomotor to promote all round development of the students. It is a school-based evaluation, which covers all aspects of school activities related to child's development. It emphasizes two-fold objectives such as continuity of evaluation and assessment of learning outcomes in a comprehensive manner. It covers all the domains of learning, i.e. cognitive, affective and psychomotor domains. It treats evaluation as a developmental process. Evaluation in the cognitive domain is associated with the evaluation of cognitive abilities such as knowledge, understanding, application, etc. Evaluation in the affective domain means evaluation of attributes such as attitudes, motives, interests and other personality traits. Evaluation in the psychomotor domain involves assessing learners' skills to use their hands (e.g. in handwriting, construction and projects).

In CCE, student's performance in both scholastic and co-scholastic activities is assessed. CCE aims to reduce the curricular workload on students and to improve the overall abilities and skill of students by means of evaluation of students' performance in both types of activities.

CCE is required to:

- suggest suitable tools and techniques for achieving continuous comprehensive evaluation;
- identify the latent talents of the students in different contexts;
- suggest ways and strategies of sensitizing school administrators, parents and the community about CCE;
- identify strategies for raising students' achievement;
- provide a holistic profile of the student through assessment of both scholastic and non-scholastic aspects of education;
- use evaluation as a tool for continuous improvement of the school and the students; and
- plan a Comprehensive Evaluation Programme for improving schools.

The objectives of CCE are:

- To help develop cognitive, psychomotor and affective skills.
- To lay emphasis on thought process and de-emphasise memorization
- To make evaluation an integral part of teaching-learning process
- To use evaluation for improvement of students' achievement and teaching-learning strategies on the basis of regular diagnosis followed by remedial instruction
- To use evaluation as a quality control devise to maintain desired standard of performance
- To determine social utility, desirability or effectiveness of a programme and take appropriate decisions about the learner, the process of learning and the learning environment
- To make the process of teaching and learning a learner-centered activity.

The nature of CCE is so comprehensive that it includes almost all aspects of child development. It integrates assessment with teaching and learning process; emphasising assessment of learner abilities in scholastic areas along with the co-scholastic areas.

- CCE encourages and motivates students to be positive in their attitudes.
- It emphasises that teacher's judgment should be made through an honest and objective appraisal without bias.
- It also encourages continuous interaction with parents with regard to their children's progress and performance.
- CCE is developmental in nature because emphasis is given on improvement of students' learning throughout the schooling process.
- It is a process of continuous attempts to assess whether desirable changes are taking place in students along the lines of educational objectives.

The features of CCE are:

(1) The 'comprehensive' component of CCE takes care of assessment of all round development of the child's personality. It includes assessment in Scholastic as well as Co-Scholastic aspects of the student's growth.

(2) Assessment in Co-Scholastic areas is done using multiple techniques on the basis of identified criteria, while assessment of personal-social qualities is done on the basis of Indicators of Assessment and Checklists.

(3) The 'continuous' aspect of CCE takes care of 'continual' and 'periodicity' aspect of evaluation.

(4) Periodicity means assessment of performance done frequently at the end of unit/term using certain standards (i.e. acceptable level of performance based on the objectives).

(5) It is school-based evaluation of students covering all aspects of students' development.

(6) Assessment in Scholastic areas is done informally and formally using multiple techniques of evaluation continually and periodically. The diagnostic evaluation takes place at the end of a unit/term as a test. The causes of poor performance and the areas of poor performance are diagnosed using diagnostic tests. These are followed with appropriate interventions followed by retesting.

(7) Continual, means assessment of students in the beginning of instructions (placement evaluation) and assessment during the instructional process (formative evaluation) done informally using multiple techniques of evaluation.

(8) Scholastic aspects include subject specific areas, whereas Co-Scholastic aspects include Personal-Social Qualities, Co-Curricular Activities, Attitudes and Values.

Q46.Enumerate and explain four areas of students process which should be covered in CCE.

Or

Explain the need and areas of evaluating socio-personal qualities (SPQ) of learners. **[April-2016, Q.No.-41]**

Or

List two areas of learner assessment under CCE.

[October-2016, Q.No.-40]

Ans. CCE shall be carried out in four areas of student progress in all the elementary classes. These are as follows:

(1) **Evaluation in Curricular Areas:** Curricular areas includes all subjects of studies at elementary level, i.e. Language, Mathematics, General Science, Social Studies; and predominantly covers the cognitive domain aiming at the intellectual development of children. The evaluation of curricular areas requires more inputs to make it more systematic. Hence, various dimensions have been identified for assessment with variations from level to level.

Evaluation in curricular areas has to be continuous from the beginning of the academic session. An academic session is divided into two phases: April to September and October to March. In each phase there shall be three assessments at an interval of two months. Each assessment shall cover the portions covered within that period only. Portions covered in one assessment shall not be repeated in another or subsequent assessments. In curricular areas there should be both formal and in-formal evaluation as a part of CCE. Assessment of students learning in these areas shall be done through teacher made unit tests. The answer papers shall be shown to the students and parents for sharing and feedback. A variety of tools/techniques shall be used in assessment, such as written, oral, assignment, project, observation etc. Further, peer evaluation and self-evaluation can also to be used as a part of informal evaluation under CCE.

(2) **Evaluation in other Curricular Areas:** Subjects like Art Education, Health and Physical Education, Peace Education and Work Education come under other curricular areas. Students taking part in Art Education, Work Education, Peace Education and Health and Physical Education should be observed and assessed by the teachers. Evaluation in these areas shall be made though project and performance, etc. However, students' learning and progress on the above areas are to be internally evaluated by the teachers in both inside and outside the classroom, while the learners doing project work in group, interacting in a group while learning collaboratively and/or performing any task in classroom. There shall be at least two assessments in each phase of academic session with the help of three point-scale (A, B, and C) at primary level; and five- point scale at upper primary level. The results of evaluation shall be shared with student and parents through report cards.

(3) **Evaluation in other Curricular Activities:** Every school organizes a variety of curricular activities to provide students with opportunities for participation, exposure, experience and building his/her capabilities/skills to promote various dimension of personality. The activities identified for different stages of education are as follows:

Curricular Activities for Classes I and II
(i)   Language skills (Recitation with action, narration of events, storytelling and drawing)
(ii)   Nature observation
(iii) Games and sports
(iv)   Other skills

Curricular Activities for Classes III to V
(i)   Language related skills (Reading/recitation, storytelling and speech)
(ii)   Scientific skill
(iii) Games and sports
(iv)   Others (mono action, dance, song, drawing)

Curricular Activities for Classes VI to VIII
(i)   Literary activities (Reading/recitation, debate, speech and creative work)
(ii)   Scientific skills (club activities, nature observation and computer literacy)
(iii) Games and sports
(iv)   Other (cultural activities, scouts and guides, first aid and Red cross)

Prior to the NCF-2005, the activities such as debate, recitation, creative writing, music, drama, dance, painting, drawing, games, sports and other outdoor and indoor activities were termed as non-scholastic, co-scholastic or co-curricular activities and were mostly neglected in schools. However, NCF-2005 has considered that all activities being organized in the schools are essentially a part of curriculum and should be considered as curricular activities. Each school should select multiple activities under each category so that each and every student gets opportunities for participation as per his/ her interest and suitability. To be a top scorer — Read only GPH Books.

(4) **Evaluation of Social and Personal Qualities (SPQ):** Students through interaction with their peers, teachers and school environment develop many Social and Personal Qualities. All such traits contribute to a student's personality. The personal and social qualities to be promoted among the students at different stages of education are as follows:

For Classes I & II
(i)   Cleanliness
(ii)   Cooperation
(iii)   Use of toilets
(iv)   Punctuality
(v)   Use of dust bin/waste basket
(vi)   Washing of hands before and after eating
(vii)   Respect towards superiors/elders
(viii) Taking care of animals/ birds and surroundings

For Classes III to V
(i)   Cleanliness
(ii)   Co operation
(iii)   Punctuality
(iv)   Environmental awareness and protection
(v)   Love for physical labor
(vi)   Respect towards superior
(vii)   Shouldering responsibility

For Classes VI & VII
(i)   Truthfulness
(ii)   Cooperation
(iii)   Emotional stability
(iv)   Punctuality
(v)   Environmental awareness
(vi)   Love for physical work/ labor
(vii)   Respect towards supervisors
(viii) Protection of environment
(ix)   Appreciation
(x)   Responsibility

(xi) Leadership

(xii) Honesty

SPQs as suggested in NCF-2005 are to observed as an integral part of curricular areas and curricular activities in each and every class; and as an elements of affective domain. Keeping in mind the maturity level of the students, the teacher shall observe the direction of development rather than its status. The teacher will observe and record SPQs using behavior indicators with the help of three-point scale – A, B, and C for primary level and five-point scale for upper primary level so as to eliminate the unhealthy competitions.

Q47.What are the objectives of teaching social sciences at primary and upper primary stage?

Ans. Following are the objectives of teaching Social Studies/Science at primary and upper primary state:

(1) Primary Stage: The objectives of teaching social sciences at the primary stage are:

(i) To develop in the child skills of observation, identification, and classification.

(ii) To develop in the child a holistic understanding of the environment with emphasis on the interrelationship of the natural and the social environments.

(iii) To sensitize the child to social issues and develop in him/her a respect for difference and diversity.

(2) Upper Primary Stage: The objectives of teaching the social sciences at the upper primary stage are:

(i) To develop an understanding about the earth as the habitat of humankind and other forms of life.

(ii) To initiate the learner in to study of her/his own region, state, and country, in the global context.

(iii) To initiate the learner in to study of her/his own region, state, and country in the global context.

(iv) To initiate the learner into a study of India's past, with references to contemporary developments in other parts of the world.

(v) To introduce the learner into a study of India's past, with references to contemporary developments in other parts of the world.

(vi) To introduce the learner to the functioning and dynamics of social and political institutions and processes of the country.

Q48.What are indicators? Also, enlist learning indicators of learning.

Or

What do you mean by indicator? Discuss the characteristics of a good indicator.

Ans. A single indicator can rarely provide useful information about such a complex phenomena as learning. Indicator usually designed to generate more and more accurate information about conditions. The purpose of indicator is to characterise the nature of system through its components- How they are related and how they change our time? This information can be used to judge progress towards some goal or standards. An indicator can:

- Set goals and priorities.
- Evaluate programme.
- Describe and state problems much clearly.

The characteristics of a good indicator are given below:

- It allows relating with the other indicators.
- Its ability to summarise information.
- It measures how far and how close one is from the objectives?
- It helps to compare its value to a standard itself.
- It provides useful information to the teachers.
- It helps to identify problematic situations.

At the elementary level, we should help students' ability to develop the following indicators:

- **Observation and Reporting:** Explores, shares, narrates and draws, picture-reading, makes pictures, collects and records information, tables and maps.

- **Discussion:** Listens, talks, expresses opinion, discovers.

- **Expression:** Expresses through gestures/body movements, expresses verbally, expresses through drawing/writing/sculpting, expresses through creative writing.

- **Explanation:** Reasoning, makes logical connections, describes events/situations and formulates one's own reasoning's, makes simple gestures, thinks critically, and makes logical connections.

- **Classification:** Identifies objects-based on observable features, identified Similarities and differences in objects, sorts/groups objects-based on observable features. Compares objects and classifies them based on physical features.

- **Questioning:** Expresses curiosity, asks questions, raises critical questions and frames questions.

- **Analysis:** Defines situations/events, identifies/predicts possible causes of any event/situation, makes hypotheses and inferences

- **Experimentation (Hands on activities)**–Improvises, makes simple things and performs simple experiments.

- **Concern for Justice and Equality:** Sensitivity towards the disadvantaged or people with disability shows concern for environment.

- **Cooperation:** Takes responsibilities and takes initiatives, shares and works together with empathy.

Q49. Define alternative assessment. What are the various alternatives of assessment?

Or

What is a rubric? Examine its any four advantages.

[October-2016, Q.No.-42]

Ans. Alternative assessment is any classroom assessment practice that focuses on continuous individual student progress. Perhaps the best way to define alternative assessment is to say that it is the counter to traditional forms of standardized assessment.

Alternative assessment procedures are based upon constructivist principles of knowledge construction. Fundamental focus of such procedures lies on learner's ability for creative expression and proficiency in real life task and activities.

Assessment in social science does not have to be limited to only paper and pencil test. Assessment can be done through drama, picture reading tasks, projects, experiments, children's drawing and even dialogues with children.

(1) Assessing through creative writing, acting and dancing: Children learn more effectively when children are given a chance for creative expression-either through acting, drawing or creative writing. It also makes it positive for us to assess their original ideas.

For example, we take the theme environmental pollution and see how assessment can be done in three ways:

    A: Conventional Questions

        (i)   Name three human activities that cause water pollution.

    B: Drawing

        (i)   Draw picture showing how water gets polluted.

    C: Creative Writing Exercise

        (i)   Describe how water of your village pond gets polluted and suggest how to prevent it.

(2) Picture reading tasks for assessment: Using pictures and photographs, various questions can be framed to give children to express their ability to observe, make connections and interpret. For example, present the paintings of different temple of our country categorizing them as painting A, painting B, painting C, ask the students to observe and to answer the following questions:

    (i)   Describe the people's love for art and music.

    (ii)   Can you guess the number of days/months/years devoted to construct temple in painting C?

    (iii)   Describe the life style (for example food habit, dress pattern) of people from painting A.

(3) Children's drawing: Through drawing, children can express themselves much more freely and deeply. It gives an opportunity to the children for personal interpretation and imagination. Children enjoy drawing. It is also a pleasurable way of asking them about their understanding about a concept or idea. Each child's drawing is different and distinct. Drawing is not only an enjoyable activity for children but a very effective learning opportunity for teachers. As we all see here, drawings help teachers in assessing children's concepts, ideas, thinking and personal feelings, which they may not to express in words.

Here, we take an example of drawing a picture of a village pond:

This drawing exercise may give us many insights into children's thinking about how water in villages gets polluted and different pollutants, etc. As an assessment exercise, this becomes an important guide for further learning.

(4) Field Visit: Field Trips are one of the oldest methods. They provide experiences, which are real and life-like. They provide the most effective avenues through which pupils become informed about their social, natural and economic environment. Field trips may be arranged to such places like a factory to explain the process of production in economics. Trips can be organised to agricultural fields to make the students understand the stages of farming.

(5) Portfolio Assessment: Use of student portfolio in learning and assessment is the recent development in the teaching-learning process. Student portfolio is a collection of important contributions of the learner recorded in a very systematic manner. The portfolio may be kept with the teacher or in the school for taking periodical or terminal decision about the learner. This is an important technique for assessing student performance in Social Sciences because Social Sciences include varieties of activities related to community and society, art and culture, democracy and values, economics and demography, etc. The important learning tasks performed by students of Social Sciences may be preserved in individual portfolios and considered for evaluation periodically, as and when required. Portfolio assessment provides an authentic basis to the teachers to go through the learning tasks performed by the learners and accordingly assess their abilities. Portfolio assessment also forms the basis for final certification of the learners.

Use of scrap files can also be a part of learner's portfolio. In scrap file, learners can paste different pictures related to the topic taught in the classroom. That can sensitise the learners and draw their attention towards the topic of discussion. For example, before teaching the theme Akbar, teacher may motivate the learners to prepare scrap file of Akbar, including the picture of Akbar, his contributions to the society, etc. That scrap file can further be kept in the portfolio for evaluation.

(6) Rubrics for Performance-Based Assessment: Performance-based assessment is especially relevant for assessing complex tasks. This type of assessment involves creating and applying a rubric, a set of statements that describe criteria for determining the level of performance for a student response. There is no "right" number of levels to use. Three to five levels are usually adequate for providing a sufficient degree of discrimination of performance.

A rubric can be specific or general in relation to a complex task. The advantage of a specific rubric is that it allows for a more precise determination of performance. The disadvantage is that a specific rubric requires significant time to create. A general rubric can be too vague, thereby requiring a high degree of subjective judgment when deciding a level of performance. This can easily lead to inconsistent determinations of levels of performance (scoring) for the various student responses. However, a general rubric is faster to create. One solution to the dilemma is to create a rubric that has qualities of a general and a specific rubric (a middle ground between the two). It is less time consuming to create and to apply, and also less likely to lead to inconsistent scoring.

Thus, we can say that rubric has following advantages:

- Improve student performance by clearly showing the students how their work will be evaluated and what is expected.

- Help students become better judges of the quality of their own work.

- Allow assessment to be more objective and consistent.

- Force the teacher to clarify his/her criteria in specific terms.

- Reduce the amount of time teachers spend evaluating student work.

- Promote student awareness about the criteria to use in assessing peer performance.

- Provide useful feedback to teacher regarding the effectiveness of the instruction.

- Provide students with more informative feedback about their strengths and areas in need of improvement.

- Are easy to use and easy to explain.

Q50.Describe grading vs. marking system in assessment.

Ans. Marking or scoring is the process of awarding a number (usually), or a symbol to represent the level of student learning achievement. The most common method is by adding up the number of correct answers on a test, and assigning a number that correlates (Sadler, 2005). Higher numbers reflect better quality work. As a rule, marking applies to students' level of performance in individual assessment tasks, not to overall achievement in a course.

Grading is the grouping of student academic work into bands of achievement. Grading usually occurs at a larger level, for example: significant assessment tasks, entire modules or courses and again is represented by a symbol (Sadler, 2005). The most common grading symbols are A,B,C,D, etc. and HD, D, C, P (High Distinction, Distinction, Credit, Pass), etc.

Marks are also a type of grades on a very big 101-point scale. A properly introduced grading system may not only provide for the comparison of students' performance, but also indicate the quality of performance. Best help books for NIOS students—GPH books.

Q51. What are the methods of assigning grades? Discuss.

Ans. There are mainly four kinds of grading, i.e. direct grading, indirect grading, absolute grading and relative grading, which are discussed as follows:

(1) Direct Grading: In direct grading, assessment of quality and range are separated. First, the teacher evaluates the quality of an answer and awards grades. Afterward, weightage is assigned, depending on the range of the question. How overall grade is arrived at from a question paper having four essay questions is given in the following table:

Table: 3.2: Grades and Grade Points as Per Question Numbering

Question No.	Grades	Grade Points
1	B	4
2	C	3
3	D	2
4	A	5

$$\text{Overall Grade} = \frac{\text{Total of Grade Points Obtained}}{\text{No. of Questions}}$$

$$= \frac{4+3+2+5}{4} = \frac{14}{4}$$

$$= \frac{14}{4}$$

$$= 3.5$$

Thus, the overall grade point is 3.5. In order to know overall grade, the following table is referred to.

Table: 3.3: Grades according to Grade Point Range

Grades	Grade Point Range
A	4.50-5.0
B	3.50-4.49
C	2.50-3.49
D	1.50-2.49
E	0-1.49

Since the overall grade point is 3.5, the overall grade is B.

(2) Indirect Grading: In indirect grading, the scores awarded are normalised for ensuring proper distribution. But the implementation of indirect grading may pose difficulties as it does not have universal academic and social acceptability.

(3) Absolute Grading: In the case of absolute grading, an institution defines certain standard (level of performance) of student's achievement in the examination or in any other co-curricular activities and associates a grade with a fixed performance level. Suppose, we have divided the examinees into five different groups on the basis of their performance. Grade 'A' will be assigned to those candidates who secure 80% and above, and will be categorised as 'outstanding'. The details of such a grading scale is presented below:

Table: 3.4: Letter Grade according to Category Description

Score	Category Description	Letter Grade
80% and above	Outstanding	Very Good
60% to 79%	First Division	Good
45% to 59%	Second Division	Average
33% to 44%	Third Division	Below Average
Below 33%	Unsatisfactory	Poor

(4) Relative Grading: In this kind of grading, students in a group are ranked on the basis of their relative level of achievement. Therefore, relative grading is the process of assigning letter grades to students on the basis of ranking them on their relative level of achievement. The institution in this case takes a prior decision as to how many students would be awarded a particular grade on the basis of their relative performance.

Table: 3.5: Relative Performance according to Grades

Grades	Relative Performance
A	Highest 10% to 20% of students
B	Higher 20% to 30% of students
C	Next 30% to 50% of students
D	Lower 10% to 20% of students
E	Lowest 0% to 10% of students

In the above example, top 10% to 20% of students will be assigned grade 'A' and bottom 0% to 10% of students will be assigned 'E' grade.

Q52. Illustrate the comparison of overall performance of students in a class.

Ans. Comparison of students' performance both within the subject and across the subjects is allowed by relative grading system. But if we want to compare the overall performance of the students in different subjects, we need to find out a Grade Point Average (GPA) by combining the grades awarded in different subjects. However, for computing the GPA, the grades in all the subjects must be based on relative grading method.

Table 3.6:

Students	Grades in Different Subjects					GPA
X	A	C	B	B	C	3.8
Y	C	B	A	A	B	4.2

$$\text{GPA of X} = \frac{5+3+4+4+3}{5} = \frac{19}{5} = 3.8$$

$$\text{GPA of Y} = \frac{3+4+5+5+4}{5} = \frac{21}{5} = 4.2$$

Thus, on this basis of GPA, it may be inferred that the performance of 'Y' is better than that of 'X'. Read GPH books and score excellent marks.

Q53. What are the guidelines for effective grading? Enlist the benefits of grading.

Ans. Following are the guidelines for effective grading by Gronlund and Linn, (1990, p.433):

(1) Describe your grading procedures to pupils at the beginning of instruction.

(2) Make clear to pupils that the course grade will be based on achievement only.

(3) Explain how other elements (effort, work habits, personal-social characteristics) will be reported.

(4) Relate the grading procedures to the intended learning outcomes (i.e. instructional objectives)

(5) Obtain valid evidence (e.g. tests, reports, ratings) as a basis for assigning grades.

(6) Take precautions to prevent cheating on tests, reports, and other types of evaluation.

(7) Return and review all test results (and other evaluation data) as soon as possible.

(8) Properly weigh the various types of achievement included in the grade.

(9) Do not lower an achievement grade for weak effort or misbehavior.

(10) Be fair, avoid bias, and when in doubt (as with a borderline score) review the evidence. If still in doubt, assign the higher grade.

Benefits of Grading: As per NCERT, 2000, pp.35-36, benefits of grading are as follows:

- It will minimize misclassification of students on the basis of unreliable marks.
- It will eliminate unhealthy cut-throat competition among high achievers.
- It will be a great relief to low achievers when the system of declaring pass/ fail is abolished.
- It will provide a chance to improve upon his/her grade in any subject over a period of time without carrying a stigma of fail.
- Students will stop committing suicides or running away from homes on failing in examinations.
- The nation will be benefited by sharing human and natural resources by not failing candidates that may be to the extent of 50% or more.

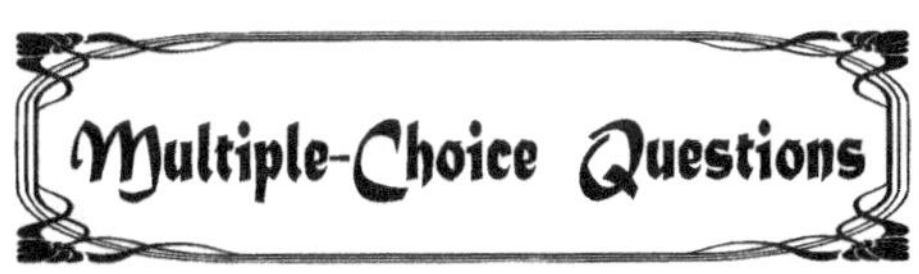

Q1. Which is the largest religious community of India?
  (a) Hindus   **(b) Muslims**
  (c) Christians   **(d) Sikhs**
Ans. (a) Hindus

Q2. **Which is the youngest religion?**
(a) **Christianity**   (b) **Hinduism**
(c) **Buddhism**   (d) **Sikhism**
Ans. (d) Sikhism

Q3. **Among the following, which one is not included in concrete operational stage?**
(a) **Classification**   (b) **Seriation**
(c) **Characterization**   (d) **Conservation**
Ans. (c) Characterization

Q4. **How many identifiable communities are there in India?**
(a) **4365**   (b) **4635**
(c) **3656**   (d) **6556**
Ans. (b) 4635

Q5. **Which of the following percentages of traits is shared by Muslims with Buddhists in India?**
(a) **91.18%**   (b) **92.18%**
(c) **93.18%**   (d) **94.18%**
Ans. (a) 91.18%

Q6. **Which step will be taken by a group of students after the step of 'Forming the groups' in project work?**
(a) **Selection of the sub theme**
(b) **Selection of a theme**
(c) **Group presentation**
(d) **Preparing for presentation**
Ans. (b) Selection of a theme

Q7. **Which one of the following is not included in the elements of cooperative learning?**
(a) **Student self-esteem**   (b) **Group Processing**
(c) **Positive Interdependence** (d) **Face-to-Face Interaction**
Ans. (a) Student self-esteem

Q8. **Which of the following skills a Social Science teacher should try to develop in his students?**
(a) **Skill to observe**   (b) **Skill to identify**
(c) **Skill to classify**   (d) **All of the above**
Ans. (b) All of the above

Q9. **Storytelling is a _________method of entertaining the children by grandparents especially by grandma.**
(a) **Untraditional**   (b) **New**
(c) **Orthodox**   (d) **Traditional**
Ans. (d) Traditional

Q10. **Planning, execution and follow up are the stages of _____.**
(a) **Field trip**   (b) **Discussion method**
(c) **Story telling**   (d) **Project method**
Ans. (a) Field trip

Q11. **Which is/are the map skill/s among the following?**
(a) **Reading colours**   (b) **Noting Directions**
(c) **Reading symbols**   (d) **All of the above**
Ans. (d) All of the above

Q12. Which of the following is not true about use of learning resources in Social Science?

(a) It makes teaching and learning effective

(b) It consumes time unnecessarily

(c) It helps in clarifying concepts

(d) It enables students to remember for longer periods

Ans. (b) It consumes time unnecessarily

Q13. The term 'Realia' refers to ______ objects from real life such as coins, tools and textiles that do not easily fit into the orderly categories of printed material.

(a) three-dimensional				(b) four-dimensional

(c) five-dimensional				(d) two-dimensional

Ans. (a) three-dimensional

Q14. Charts are used to convey both______ messages.

(a) non-verbal and graphic			(b) numeric and graphic

(c) verbal and graphic				(d) None of the above

Ans. (c) verbal and graphic

Q15. What is the purpose of assessment?

(a) To improve teaching-learning process

(b) To improve student's behaviour

(c) To improve school's curriculum

(d) To improve teaching skills

Ans. (a) To improve teaching-learning process

Q16. Effective recording is done by which of the following points?

(a) Preparing a child's profile

(b) Making note of important changes

(c) Assessing the child's work during an activity

(d) All of the above

Ans. (d) All of the above

Q17. What is the full form of CCE?

(a) Commerial and Comprehensive Evaluation

(b) Continuous and Comprehensive Evaluation

(c) Continuous and Comprehensive Examination

(d) Central and Comprehensive Evaluation

Ans. (b) Continuous and Comprehensive Evaluation

Q18. RTE Act was implemented in the year______.

(a) 2008

(b) 2009

(c) 2012

(d) 2014

Ans. (b) 2009

Q19. What is the advantage of 'Rubrics'?

(a) Allow assessment to be more objective and consistent.

(b) Easy to use and easy to explain.

(c) Reduce the amount of time teachers spend evaluating student work.

(d) All of the above

Ans. (d) All of the above

Q20. According to 2011 census, the Union Territory of India with lowest literacy rate is:

(a) Chandigarh

(b) Pondicherry

(c) Andaman & Nicobar Islands

(d) Dadra & Nagar Haveli

Ans. (d) Dadra & Nagar Haveli

☺☺☺

Gullybaba Publishing House Pvt. Ltd.

ISO 9001 & ISO 14001 Certified Co.

We will help you to write and share it with world

Question Papers

DIPLOMA IN ELEMENTARY EDUCATION [D.EL.ED.]
(Learning Social Science at Upper Primary Level)
(उच्च प्राथमिक स्तर पर सामाजिक विज्ञान शिक्षा)

(509)
April -2016

Note: (i) Attempt all questions.

(ii) Marks are indicated against each question.

निर्देश : (i) सभी प्रश्नों के उत्तर दीजिए।

(ii) प्रत्येक प्रश्न के सामने उसके अंक दिए गए हैं।

Question Nos. **1** to **15** are multiple-choice questions. Choose the correct answer from the four alternatives (A), (B), (C) and (D) given against each question and write the correct answer in your answer-book:

प्रश्न संख्या 1 से 15 बहु-विकल्पीय प्रश्न हैं। निम्नलिखित प्रश्नों में प्रत्येक के चार विकल्प दिए गए हैं। इन चार विकल्पों (क), (ख), (ग) और (घ) में से सही उत्तर चुनकर अपनी उत्तर-पुस्तिका में लिखिए:

Q1. Which of the following States is having the highest literacy rate?
(A) Bihar
(B) Rajasthan
(C) Kerala
(D) Jharkhand

निम्नलिखित राज्यों में से किसमें साक्षरता की दर अधिकतम है?

(क) बिहार

(ख) राजस्थान

(ग) केरल

(घ) झारखण्ड

Ans. (C) Kerala

Q2. "History is the story of men living in societies." Who said this?
(A) Prof. Maitland
(B) Prof. Renier
(C) Prof. Ghose
(D) Henry Johnson

"इतिहास समुदायों में रहने वाले व्यक्तियों की कहानी है।" यह किसने कहा?

(क) प्रोफेसर मैटलैण्ड

(ख) प्रोफेसर रेनियर

(ग) प्रोफेसर घोष

(घ) हेनरी जॉनसन

Ans. (B) Prof. Renier

Q3. In _____ approach, a phenomenon is studied as whole.
(A) systematic
(B) regional
(C) political
(D) physical

........उपागम में एक तत्त्व का संपूर्ण अध्ययन किया जाता है।

(क) क्रमबद्ध

(ख) प्रादेशिक

(ग) राजनैतिक

(घ) भौतिक

Ans. (A) systematic

Q4. "The Social Studies in concerned with man and his interaction with his social and physical environment..." is the definition given by
(A) John V. Michaela
(B) James High
(C) Charles Beard
(D) S. K. Kochhar

"सामाजिक अध्ययन मनुष्य से एवं मनुष्य का उसके सामाजिक तथा भौतिक वातावरण के साथ संबंधों से संबंधित है..." परिभाषा दी गई है

(क) जॉन वी. माइकेला द्वारा

(ख) जेम्स हाई द्वारा

(ग) चार्ल्स बियर्ड द्वारा

(घ) एस. के. कोचर द्वारा

Ans. (A) John V. Michaela

Q5. The Social Science originated in _____ century.
(A) twenty-first
(B) twentieth
(C) nineteenth
(D) eighteenth

सामाजिक विज्ञान का उदय........सदी में हुआ।

(क) इक्कीसवीं

(ख) बीसवीं

(ग) उन्नीसवीं

(घ) अठारहवीं

Ans. (D) eighteenth

Q6. The Indus Valley Civilization had flourished at
(A) northern part
(B) southern part
(C) eastern part
(D) western part

सिंधु घाटी सभ्यता........ में पनपी थी।

(क) उत्तरी भाग

(ख) दक्षिणी भाग

(ग) पूर्वी भाग

(घ) पश्चिमी भाग

Ans. (D) western part

Q7. Which one of the following is not a part of society?
(A) Family
(B) Community
(C) People
(D) Land

निम्न में से कौन समाज का अंग नहीं है?

(क) परिवार

(ख) समुदाय

(ग) लोग

(घ) भूमि

Ans. (D) Land

Q8. Which teaching strategy is best to clarify the location of Delhi?
(A) Role play
(B) Discussion
(C) Lecture method
(D) Map-based

दिल्ली की अवस्थिति को स्पष्ट करने के लिए कौन-सी शिक्षण रणनीति उत्तम है?

(क) कला अभिनय

(ख) चर्चा करना

(ग) व्याख्यान विधि

(घ) मानचित्र-आधारित

Ans. (D) Map-based

Q9. **Which one of the following is not included in Political Geography?**
(A) **Physical features**
(B) **States**
(C) **Nation**
(D) **Political parties**

निम्न में से कौन राजनैतिक भूगोल में सम्मिलित नहीं है?

(क) भौतिक लक्षण

(ख) राज्य

(ग) राष्ट्र

(घ) राजनैतिक दल

Ans. (D) Political parties

Q10. **The disadvantage of problem-solving method is**
(A) **principles of learning**
(B) **democratic way of life**
(C) **spending time and money**
(D) **developing problem-solving skills**

समस्या-समाधान विधि का दोष है

(क) सीखने का सिद्धांत

(ख) लोकतांत्रिक जीवन का तरीका

(ग) समय व पैसे का खर्च

(घ) समस्या-समाधान कौशल का विकास

Ans. (C) spending time and money

Q11. **Identify the subject area from the following which is *not* included in Social Science at upper primary level:**
(A) **History**
(B) **Psychology**
(C) **Political Science**
(D) **Geography**

निम्न में से उस विषय की पहचान कीजिए जो उच्च प्राथमिक स्तर पर सामाजिक विज्ञान का अंग नहीं है:

(क) इतिहास

(ख) मनोविज्ञान

(ग) राजनैतिक विज्ञान

(घ) भूगोल

Ans. (B) Psychology

Q12. **Continuous and comprehensive evaluation in education includes**
(A) **formative evaluation only**

(B) both formative and summative evaluation
(C) summative evaluation only
(D) None of the above

शिक्षा में सतत एवं व्यापक मूल्यांकन में सम्मिलित है

(क) केवल रचनात्मक मूल्यांकन

(ख) रचनात्मक व योगात्मक दोनों मूल्यांकन

(ग) केवल योगात्मक मूल्यांकन

(घ) उपर्युक्त में से कोई नहीं

Ans. (D) None of the above

Q13. **NCF (2005) suggests ____ for Social Science at upper primary level.**
(A) multi-disciplinary approach
(B) field approach
(C) theoretical approach
(D) reading approach

राष्ट्रीय पाठ्यक्रम रूपरेखा (2008) में उच्च प्राथमिक स्तर पर सामाजिक विज्ञान हेतु ....का सुझाव दिया गया है।

(क) बहु-विषयक उपागम

(ख) क्षेत्र उपागम

(ग) सैद्धांतिक उपागम

(घ) पढ़ने का उपागम

Ans. (A) multi-disciplinary approach

Q14. **The term 'Realia' means**
(A) three-dimensional objective
(B) two-dimensional objective
(C) one-dimensional objective
(D) none of the above

'रियलिया' **(Realia)** का अर्थ है

(क) त्रि-आयामी उद्देश्य

(ख) द्वि-आयामी उद्देश्य

(ग) एकल-आयामी उद्देश्य

(घ) उपर्युक्त में से कोई नहीं

Ans. (A) three-dimensional objective

Q15. **RTE Act was implemented in the year_____.**
(A) 2008
(B) 2009
(C) 2012
(D) 2014

शिक्षा का अधिकार अधिनियम वर्ष....... में लागू हुआ।

(क) 2008

(ख) 2009

(ग) 2012

(घ) 2014

Ans. (B) 2009

Answer Question Nos. 16 to 30 as directed:

प्रश्न संख्या 16 से 30 तक के उत्तर निर्देशानुसार दीजिए:

Q16. Write the name of the author of the book entitled, *Spirit of the Laws.*

'स्पिरिट ऑफ द लॉस' *(Spirit of the Laws)* शीर्षक पुस्तक के लेखक का नाम लिखिए।

Ans. Montesquieu is the author of the book entitled *Spirit of the Laws.*

Q17. The Social Science became a part of school curriculum in India from____ century.

(Fill in the blank)

भारत में सामाजिक विज्ञान विद्यालय पाठ्यक्रम का अंग.......सदी में बना।

(रिक्त स्थान भरिए)

Ans. eighteenth

Q18. Herodotus is popularly known as _____.

(Fill in the blank)

हिरोडोटस आमतौर पर...... जाने जाते हैं।

(रिक्त स्थान भरिए)

Ans. 'Father of History'

Q19. Ten core components of curriculum were outlined in which document?

पाठ्यचर्या के दस मुख्य घटकों की रूपरेखा किस दस्तावेज में दी गई थी?

Ans. In 1988, the NCERT brought out National Curriculum Framework for Elementary and Secondary Education on the basis of National Policy on Education, 1986. The Minimum Levels of Learning (MLL) and ten core components were emphasized in this document.

Q20. Which Commission considered strengthening of social and national integration as one of the major goals of education?

किस आयोग ने सामाजिक एवं राष्ट्रीय एकीकरण को शिक्षण के मुख्य उद्देश्यों में से एक रूप में संस्तुत किया था?

Ans. The Indian Education Commission (1964-66) considered strengthening of social and national integration as one of the major goals of education.

Q21. Define the term 'history'

'इतिहास' को परिभाषित कीजिए।

Ans. Refer to Chapter-2, Q.No.-1

Q22. How many languages are used in India?

भारत में कितनी भाषाओं का प्रयोग किया जाता है?

Ans. Refer to Chapter-3, Q.No.-1

Q23. Who said that 'the way children learn is by internalizing the activities, habits, dictionary and ideas of the members of the community in which they grow up...'?

किसने कहा कि 'गतिविधियों, आदतों, शब्दकोश और बच्चे जिस समुदाय में बढ़ते हैं उस समुदाय के विचारों के अंतःकरण के द्वारा बच्चा सीखता है...'?

Ans. Lev Vygotsky

Q24. Mention any *one* modern approach of teaching of Political Science.

राजनैतिक विज्ञान शिक्षण के किसी एक आधुनिक उपागम का वर्णन कीजिए।

Ans. Chapter-2, Q.No.-16

Q25. Write any *one* feature of a multi-graded class.

बहु-श्रेणी कक्षा की कोई एक विशेषता लिखिए।

Ans. The attractive feature of multi-grade system in class is its close participation, cultural diversity and multifariousness. Composite classes or multi-graded classes provide a range of levels of work, so the needs of both talented children and slower learners can be catered for, while providing a supportive environment for both.

Q26. Define the term 'Globe'.

'ग्लोब' को परिभाषित कीजिए।

Ans. Refer to Chapter-3, Q.No.-28

Q27. What is the meaning of 'Diorama'?

'डायोरमा' (Diorama) का अर्थ क्या है?

Ans. Refer to Chapter-3, Q.No.-27

Q28. Write any *one* use of Internet.

इंटरनेट का कोई एक उपयोग लिखिए।

Ans. Refer to Chapter-3, Q.No.-36

Q29. Define 'map scale'.

'मानचित्र मापनी' का अर्थ लिखिए।

Ans. Refer to Chapter-3, Q.No.-25

Q30. Subjects placed under a separate category, namely other curricular areas are___.

(Fill in the blank)

पृथक् वर्ग में रखे, जिसे अन्य पाठ्यचर्या क्षेत्र के नाम से जाना जाता है के अंतर्गत आने वाले विषय हैं.......।

(रिक्त स्थान भरिए)

Ans. Art education, Health and Physical education and Work education.

Answer Question Nos. 31 to 40 briefly:

प्रश्न संख्या 31 से 40 तक के उत्तर संक्षेप में दीजिए:

Q31. Define the relationship between Social Studies and Social Science in two points.

सामाजिक अध्ययन एवं सामाजिक विज्ञान के मध्य संबंध को दो बिंदुओं में परिभाषित कीजिए।

Ans. Refer to Chapter-1, Q.No.-3

Q32. Examine *two* literary sources of history.

इतिहास के दो साहित्यिक स्रोतों का परीक्षण कीजिए।

Ans. Refer to Chapter-2, Q.No.-5

Q33. Name any *two* contributors of traditional approach in Political Science.

राजनैतिक विज्ञान के परंपरागत उपागम में योगदान देने वालों में से कोई दो नाम लिखिए।

Ans. Socrates and Plato are two contributors of traditional approach in Political Science.

Q34. Study the table given below and answer the following questions:

Place	Adampur	Delhi	Mumbai	Una	Shimla
Temperature ($^\circ$C)	-2	18	20	2	0

(a) Which place has lowest temperature?

(b) Name the place having highest temperature.

नीचे दी गई तालिका का अध्ययन कीजिए और निम्नलिखित प्रश्नों के उत्तर दीजिए:

स्थान	आदमपुर	दिल्ली	मुम्बई	ऊना	शिमला
तापमान ($^\circ$C)	-2	18	20	2	0

(क) किस स्थान का तापमान न्यूनतम है?

(ख) उच्चतम तापमान वाले स्थान का नाम लिखिए।

Ans. (a) Adampur has lowest temperature.

(b) Mumbai has highest temperature.

Q35. Write the nature of Social Science at elementary level in two points.

प्रारंभिक स्तर पर सामाजिक विज्ञान की प्रकृति पर दो बिंदु लिखिए।

Ans. At the lower primary school level (i.e., class I-V), social sciences are taught to the learners as the part of environmental studies or environmental sciences curriculum. At this level, social science is typically organized and taught in an integrative and interdisciplinary fashion

Q36. Discuss briefly the *two* approaches to study Geography.

भूगोल के अध्ययन के दो उपागमों की संक्षेप में चर्चा कीजिए।

Ans. Refer to Chhapter-2, Q.No.-10

Q37. **Name any *two* objectives of social and political life at school level.**

विद्यालय स्तर पर सामाजिक एवं राजनैतिक जीवन के किन्हीं दो उद्देश्यों के नाम बताइए।

Ans. Refer to Chapter-2, Q.No.-19

Q38. **Write briefly the process of story-telling approach at upper primary level.**

उच्च प्राथमिक स्तर पर कहानी-कहना उपागम की प्रक्रिया को संक्षेप में लिखिए।

Ans. Refer to Chapter-2, Q.No.-21

Q39. **Suggest any *two* objectives of assessment of learner.**

विद्यार्थी के आकलन के किन्हीं दो उद्देश्यों को सुझाइए।

Ans. Refer to Chapter-3, Q.No.-40

Q40. **Mention any *two* uses of maps.**

मानचित्र के किन्हीं दो उपागमों का वर्णन कीजिए।

Ans. Refer to Chapter-3, Q.No.-24

Answer the following questions (in *500* words each):

निम्नलिखित प्रश्नों के उत्तर दीजिए (प्रत्येक *500* शब्दों में):

Q41. **Explain the need and areas of evaluating socio-personal qualities (SPQ) of learners.**

विद्यार्थियों के सामाजिक-वैयक्तिक गुणों (SPQ) के मूल्यांकन की आवश्यकता एवं क्षेत्रों की व्याख्या कीजिए।

Ans. Refer to Chapter-3, Q.No.-46

Q42. **Write any *five* differences between Social Science and Social Studies at upper primary level.**

उच्च प्राथमिक स्तर पर सामाजिक विज्ञान एवं सामाजिक अध्ययन में किन्हीं पाँच अंतरों को लिखिए।

Ans. Refer to Chapter-1, Q.No.-3

☺☺☺

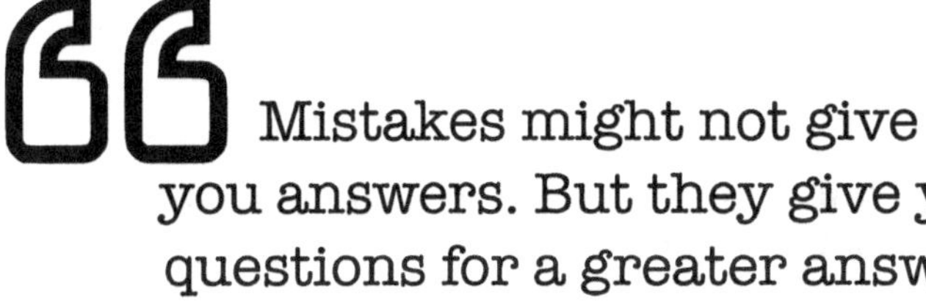

DIPLOMA IN ELEMENTARY EDUCATION [D.EL.ED.]
(Learning Social Science at Upper Primary Level)
(उच्च प्राथमिक स्तर पर सामाजिक विज्ञान शिक्षा)

(509)
October -2016

Note: (i) Attempt all questions.

   (ii) Marks are indicated against each question.

निर्देश : (i) सभी प्रश्नों के उत्तर दीजिए।

   (ii) प्रत्येक प्रश्न के सामने उसके अंक दिए गए हैं।

Question Nos. **1** to **15** are multiple-choice questions. Choose the correct answer from the four alternatives (A), (B), (C) and (D) given against each question and write the correct answer in your answer-book:

प्रश्न संख्या 1 से 15 बहु-विकल्पीय प्रश्न हैं। निम्नलिखित प्रश्नों में प्रत्येक के चार विकल्प दिए गए हैं। इन चार विकल्पों (क), (ख), (ग) और (घ) में से सही उत्तर चुनकर अपनी उत्तर-पुस्तिका में लिखिए:

Q1. In which year, the French Revolution took place?
 (A) 1769
(B) 1779
(C) 1789
(D) 1799

  फ्रांस की क्रांति किस वर्ष में हुई थी?

(क) 1769

(ख) 1779

(ग) 1789

(घ) 1799

Ans. (C) 1789

Q2. Which of the following books was written by J. G. Herder?
(A) Idea Towards a Philosophy of History
(B) Wealth of Nations
(C) Spirit of Law
(D) None of the above

  जे. जी. हर्डर ने निम्न में से कौन-सी पुस्तक लिखी थी?

(क) आइडिया टुवर्ड्स ए फिलोसॉफी ऑफ हिस्ट्री

(ख) वेल्थ ऑफ नेशंस

(ग) स्पिरिट ऑफ लॉ

(घ) उपर्युक्त में से कोई नहीं

Ans. (A) Idea Towards a Philosophy of History

Q3. Which of the following ruined cities of Indus Valley Civilization was discovered by R. D. Banerjee?

(A) Harappa

(B) Mohenjodaro

(C) Chanhudaro

(D) Lothal

आर. डी. बैनर्जी ने निम्न में से किस सिंधु घाटी के खंडहर बन चुके नगर को खोजा था?

(क) हड़प्पा

(ख) मोहनजोदाड़ो

(ग) चन्हूदड़ो

(घ) लोथल

Ans. (B) Mohenjodaro

Q4. In which of the following years, James Prinsep succeeded in deciphering an ancient inscription on a large stone pillar in Delhi?

(A) 1817

(B) 1827

(C) 1837

(D) 1847

दिल्ली के विशाल प्रस्तर स्तंभ पर लिखे हुए प्राचीन शिलालेख को पढ़ने में जेम्स प्रिंसेप ने निम्न में से किस वर्ष में सफलता पाई थी?

(क) 1817

(ख) 1827

(ग) 1837

(घ) 1847

Ans. (C) 1837

Q5. In which year, the Santhal uprising took place in India?

(A) 1855

(B) 1865

(C) 1875

(D) 1885

भारत में संथाल विद्रोह निम्न में से किस वर्ष में हुआ था?

(क) 1855

(ख) 1865

(ग) 1875

(घ) 1885

Ans. (A) 1855

Q6. Which of the following causes has worsened the condition of Indian women most?

(A) Religiousness

(B) Obsession for the male child

(C) Caste system

(D) None of the above

भारतीय नारी की स्थिति को निम्न में से किस कारण ने सबसे अधिक बिगाड़ा?

(क) धार्मिकता

(ख) पुरुष बच्चे की कामना के प्रति झुकाव

(ग) जाति-प्रथा

(घ) उपर्युक्त में से कोई नहीं

Ans. (B) Obsession for the male child

Q7. The history of Mahajanapadas is given in the textbook of which of the following classes in Central Board of Secondary Education of India?

(A) VI

(B) VII

(C) VIII

(D) None of the above

भारत के केंद्रीय माध्यमिक शिक्षा बोर्ड की निम्न में से किस कक्षा की पाठ्यपुस्तक में महाजनपदों का इतिहास है?

(क) VI

(ख) VII

(ग) VIII

(घ) उपर्युक्त में से कोई नहीं

Ans. (A) VI

Q8. Which of the following branches of Geography deals with geographical characteristics of animals and their habitats?

(A) Plant Geography

(B) Ecology

(C) Environmental Geography

(D) Zoo Geography

जीवों के अधिवास तथा उनके भौगोलिक चरित्र का अध्ययन भूगोल की निम्न में से किस शाखा में किया जाता है?

(क) पादप भूगोल

(ख) पारिस्थितिकी

(ग) पर्यावरणीय भूगोल

(घ) प्राणि भूगोल

Ans. (D) Zoo Geography

Q9. Who among the following is not considered as founding father of Sociology?

(A) Auguste Comte

(B) Grant Duff

(C) Herbert Spencer

(D) Karl Marx

निम्न में से किसको समाजशास्त्र का जनक नहीं माना जाता है?

(क) ऑगस्ट काम्टे

(ख) ग्रांट डफ

(ग) हर्बर्ट स्पेन्सर

(घ) कार्ल मार्क्स

Ans. (B) Grant Duff

Q10. Durkheim was the champion in using which of the following methods in studying the social phenomena?

(A) Historical approach

(B) Comparative approach

(C) Functionalist approach

(D) Statistical approach

सामाजिक घटनाओं के अध्ययन में दुर्खीम को निम्न में से किस विधि में महारत

हासिल थी?

(क) ऐतिहासिक उपागम

(ख) तुलनात्मक उपागम

(ग) प्रकार्यवादी उपागम

(घ) सांख्यिकीय उपागम

Ans. (C) Functionalist approach

Q11. Which of the following percentages of traits is shared by Muslims with Buddhists in India?

(A) 91·18%

(B) 92·18%

(C) 93·18%

(D) 94·18%

भारत के बौद्ध निम्न में से कितने प्रतिशत गुणों को मुसलमानों के साथ साझा

करते हैं?

(क) 91·18%

(ख) 92·18%

(ग) 93·18%

(घ) 94·18%

Ans. (A) 91·18%

Q12. **Which of the following skills a Social Science teacher should try to develop in his students?**

(A) **Skill to observe**

(B) **Skill to identify**

(C) **Skill to classify**

(D) **All of the above**

एक सामाजिक विज्ञान के शिक्षक को अपने छात्रों में निम्न में से किस कौशल को विकसित करने का प्रयास करना चाहिए?

(क) अवलोकन का कौशल

(ख) पहचानने का कौशल

(ग) वर्गीकरण का कौशल

(घ) उपर्युक्त सभी

Ans. (D) All of the above

Q13. **Which of the following statements is true about the discussion method of teaching Social Science?**

(A) **It allows every student to discuss**

(B) **It hampers collective decision**

(C) **It suppresses democratic values**

(D) **It does not seek agreement**

सामाजिक विज्ञान शिक्षण की विचार विमर्श विधि के संदर्भ में निम्न में से कौन-सा वक्तव्य सही है?

(क) यह सभी विद्यार्थियों को विचार विमर्श की अनुमति देती है

(ख) यह सामूहिक निर्णय को प्रतिबाधित करती है

(ग) यह प्रजातांत्रिक मूल्यों का दमन करती है

(घ) यह सहमति नहीं चाहती है

Ans. (A) It allows every student to discuss

Q14. **Which of the following is not true about use of learning resources in Social Science?**

(A) **It makes teaching and learning effective**

(B) **It consumes time unnecessarily**

(C) **It helps in clarifying concepts**

(D) **It enables students to remember for longer periods**

सामाजिक विज्ञान में अधिगम संसाधनों के प्रयोग के बारे में निम्न में से कौन-सा वक्तव्य सही नहीं है?

(क) ये शिक्षण तथा अधिगम को प्रभावशाली बनाते हैं

(ख) ये व्यर्थ में समय नष्ट करते हैं

(ग) ये प्रत्ययों को स्पष्ट करने में सहायता करते हैं

(घ) छात्रों द्वारा तथ्यों को लंबे समय तक याद रखने में ये सहायक होते हैं

Ans. (B) It consumes time unnecessarily

Q15. Which of the following is not subject area in assessing life skills of a student under CCE of CBSE?

(A) Thinking skill
(B) Social skill
(C) Emotional skill
(D) Art education

केंद्रीय माध्यमिक शिक्षा बोर्ड के सतत एवं व्यापक मूल्यांकन के अंतर्गत जीवन कौशल के मूल्यांकन में निम्न में से कौन-सा एक विषय-क्षेत्र नहीं है?

(क) वैचारिक कौशल

(ख) सामाजिक कौशल

(ग) भावनात्मक कौशल

(घ) कला शिक्षा

Ans. (D) Art education

Answer Question Nos. 16 to 30 :
प्रश्न संख्या 16 से 30 तक के उत्तर दीजिए:

Q16. Write the composition of Social Science.
सामाजिक विज्ञान की संरचना लिखिए।

Ans. Social Science include large number of subjects like history, political science, sociology, anthropology, economics, etc.

Q17. By what name the present society is called by the people?
आजकल का समाज लोगों द्वारा किस नाम से जाना जाता है?

Ans. 'Modern' or 'post-modern'.

Q18. What is meant by a differentiated society?
विभेदीकृत समाज से आप क्या समझते हैं?

Ans. A differentiated society is a heterogeneous and complex society which faces many social problems and challenges. The present society is a differentiated society where large number of social problems are found.

Q19. How are the subjects of Social Science linked with each other?
सामाजिक विज्ञान के विषय एक-दूसरे से किस प्रकार जुड़े हुए हैं?

Ans. Social science subjects are related with each other because human relationship is a common denominator of all the social science subjects.

Q20. Mention one measure by which we can head smoothly towards gender equality.

लैंगिक समानता की ओर सुचारु रूप से ले जाने वाले एक उपाय का उल्लेख कीजिए।

Ans. To achieve gender equality in education, we can make arrangements for quality inclusive education for girls.

Q21. Economics enables students with which efficiencies?

अर्थशास्त्र विद्यार्थियों को किन योग्यताओं से समृद्ध करता है?

Ans. Economics enable the child to be familiar with economic activities like production, consumption, distribution, exchange, etc.

Q22. Name any one form of literary sources which is helpful in constructing the history.

किसी एक प्रकार के साहित्यिक स्रोत का नाम लिखिए जो इतिहास की रचना में सहायक हो।

Ans. Sacred or religious literature

Q23. Mention two approaches to study Geography.

भूगोल के अध्ययन के दो उपागमों का उल्लेख कीजिए।

Ans. Refer to Chapter-2, Q.No.-10

Q24. Define cartography.

मानचित्रकारी को परिभाषित कीजिए।

Ans. Cartography is the art, science and technology of map making.

Q25. Explain global positioning system.

वैश्विक स्थिति प्रणाली को समझाइए।

Ans. Global Positioning System (GPS) is a space-based global navigation satellite system (GNSS) that provides location and time information in all weather, anywhere on or near the Earth, where there is an unobstructed line of sight to four or more GPS satellites.

Q26. Why is it necessary to relate new information with prior knowledge? Give one reason.

नई जानकारी को पुराने ज्ञान से जोड़ना क्यों आवश्यक होता है? एक कारण बताइए।

Ans. Refer to Chapter-3, Q.No.-5

Q27. Define the principle of purpose of project method.

परियोजना विधि के उद्देश्य के सिद्धांत को परिभाषित कीजिए।

Ans. Refer to Chapter-3, Q.No.-12

Q28. What is E-learning?

ई-लर्निंग क्या होती है?

Ans. E-learning is an instruction delivered on computer by the use of CD-ROM, Internet or Intranet. It is simply learning with the help of computer and internet technology. E-Learning is web based training with inputs of techniques such as animations, visualizations, simulation and games, text, audio, video and lots of creativity.

Q29. Mention one way by which teacher can be enriched in his subject and latest technologies.

एक शिक्षक को उसके विषय तथा उसकी नवीनतम तकनीकी से समृद्ध करने के लिए एक मार्ग का उल्लेख कीजिए।

Ans. A teacher must enrich her/his intellectual resources from time to time. For this, s/he has to attend national seminars, conferences, symposia, etc., to update her/his knowledge and skills. S/he must read the latest books, journals, magazines, etc. to keep abreast of the latest developments in the area of study.

Q30. Write any one purpose of assessment of children.

विद्यार्थियों के मूल्यांकन का कोई एक उद्देश्य लिखिए।

Ans. Refer to Chapter-3, Q.No.-40

Answer Question Nos. 31 to 40 briefly :

प्रश्न संख्या 31 से 40 तक के उत्तर संक्षेप में दीजिए:

Q31. Mention any two core components of human behaviour.

मानव व्यवहार के किन्हीं दो केंद्रीय घटकों का उल्लेख कीजिए।

Ans. Political behaviour and cultural behaviour are two core components of human behaviour.

Q32. Why is Social Science included in school curriculum? Give two reasons.

विद्यालयी पाठ्यक्रम में सामाजिक विज्ञान को क्यों सम्मिलित किया गया है? दो कारण दीजिए।

Ans. Since social sciences have great relevance for modern day society, so, they form an important component/part of modern day education/curriculum system. Social sciences have become the part of university/higher education system across the world starting from the eighteenth century. Realising the importance of social sciences for developing healthy social and democratic citizenship qualities of individuals, they have been included in the school curriculum of most of the countries of the world especially from the twentieth century either in the name of 'social studies' or in the name of 'social sciences'.

Q33. Mention two national concerns which find place in Social Science curriculum.

सामाजिक विज्ञान के पाठ्यक्रम में स्थान पाने वाले दो राष्ट्रीय संदर्भों के नाम लिखिए।

Ans. National concerns like poverty and illiteracy have found place in Social Science curriculum.

Q34. Give two reasons for why the Survey of India was established by the British.

ब्रिटिशों द्वारा सर्वे ऑफ इंडिया की स्थापना क्यों की गई? दो कारण बताइए।

Ans. Following are the two reasons for why the Survey of India was established by the British:

(1) To explore the country bit by bit.

(2)   To carry out mapping operation for military as well as civilian purposes.

Q35.Mention two types of sources in history on the basis of evidence.

साक्ष्यों पर आधारित इतिहास के दो प्रकार के स्रोतों का उल्लेख कीजिए।

Ans. Refer to Chapter-2, Q.No.-5

Q36.Examine the process of concept formation.

संकल्पना निर्माण की प्रक्रिया का परीक्षण कीजिए।

Ans. Refer to Chapter-3, Q.No.-7

Q37. Define cooperative learning.

सहयोगी अधिगम को परिभाषित कीजिए।

Ans. Refer to Chapter-3, Q.No.-16

Q38. What are organization charts?

संगठनात्मक चार्ट्स क्या होते हैं?

Ans. Refer to Chapter-3, Q.No.-30

Q39.Explain two uses of time lines in teaching historical aspects of Social Science.

सामाजिक विज्ञान के ऐतिहासिक पहलुओं के शिक्षण में कालरेखा के दो उपयोग समझाइए।

Ans. Refer to Chapter-3, Q.No.-31

Q40. List two areas of learner assessment under CCE.

सतत एवं व्यापक मूल्यांकन के अंतर्गत विद्यार्थियों के मूल्यांकन के दो क्षेत्र लिखिए।

Ans. Refer to Chapter-3, Q.No.-46

Answer the following questions (in *500* words each):

निम्नलिखित प्रश्नों के उत्तर दीजिए (प्रत्येक *500* शब्दों में)

Q41. Explain any five objectives of learning about social and political life as part of Social Science curriculum at upper primary level.

उच्च प्राथमिक स्तर पर सामाजिक विज्ञान पाठ्यक्रम के अंतर्गत सामाजिक तथा राजनीतिक जीवन के अधिगम के कोई पाँच उद्देश्य समझाइए।

Ans. Refer to Chapter-2, Q.No.-19

Q42. What is a rubric? Examine its any four advantages.

रूब्रिक क्या होता है? इसके किन्हीं चार लाभों का परीक्षण कीजिए।

Ans. Refer to Chapter-3, Q.No.-49

☺☺☺

Why Students Choose GPH Books ?

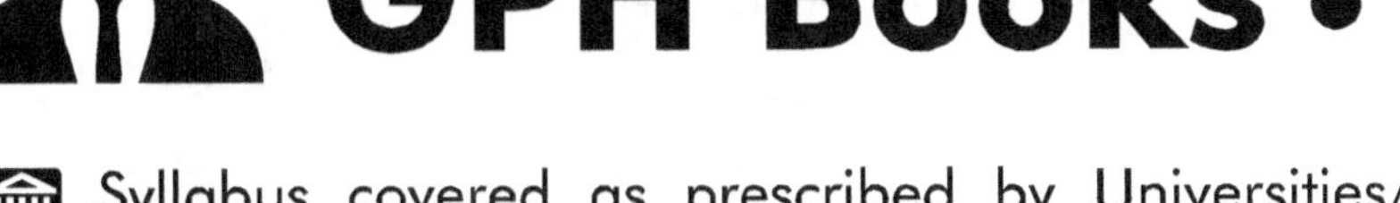

- Syllabus covered as prescribed by Universities/Boards/Institutions.

- Easily understandable language and format that help students prepare for exam in short period of time.

- Published with exam-oriented approach, hence prepared in question-answer format which provides students the instant understanding of a correct answer.

- Maximum solved previous year question papers included which help students to understand unique examination structure and equip them better for exam.

- Both semesters' question papers (June-December) are included with solutions.

- Instant updation of data as and when any change occurs.

- Use of recycled paper.

- Handy books and reasonable prices.

- For every book sold, we contribute for society/institution/NGOs/underprivileged

Why Name Gullybaba?

® Gullybaba is a combination of two significant words 'Gully' & 'Baba'. The word 'Gully' comes from the ancient game played in Rural India–Tip cat. In Hindi, we call it Gully Danda (गुल्ली डंडा) which is a great symbol of Focus & Force. The word 'Baba' stands for Respect & Honour. And these are the fundamental parameters for achieving success. Focus & Force are required to help one go a long way in life. This is all about achieving excellence in education and giving respect & honour to everyone, and thus, the name 'Gullybaba'.

To know more about why name GullyBaba visit: GullyBaba.com/why-name-gullybaba.html

Feedback

Although, we make every effort to ensure that there are no errors in GPH books. However, if you want to point out and suggest any error or want any improvement in any of our books, please let us know so that we could rectify as soon as possible. Your feedback may save hours of frustration for other readers and at the same time you will be helping students to get even higher quality study materials. Your criticisms/suggestions are highly welcomed.

NOTES